exploring

THE BASICS OF DRAWING

Victoria Vebell

THOMSON

DELMAR LEARNING

Australia Canada Mexico Singapore Spain United Kingdom United States

THOMSON

™

DELMAR LEARNING

Exploring The Basics of Drawing
Victoria Vebell

Vice President, Technology and Trades SBU:

Alar Elken

Editorial Director:

Sandy Clark

Senior Acquisitions Editor:

James Gish

Development Editor:

Jaimie Wetzel

Marketing Director:

Dave Garza

Channel Manager:

William Lawrensen

Marketing Coordinator:

Mark Pierro

Production Director:

Mary Ellen Black

Production Manager:

Larry Main

Production Editor:

Thomas Stover

Editorial Assistant:

Niamh Matthews

Art & Design Specialist:

Rachel Baker

Development:

Jan Gallagher

Cover Design:

Steven Brower

Cover Production:

David Arsenault

Cover Image:

Victoria Vebell

COPYRIGHT 2005 by Thomson Delmar Learning. Thomson, the Star Logo, and Delmar Learning are trademarks used herein under license.

Printed in the United States
3 4 5 XXX 07 06 05

For more information contact Delmar Learning
Executive Woods
5 Maxwell Drive, PO Box 8007, Clifton Park, NY 12065-8007
Or find us on the World Wide Web at
www.delmarlearning.com

ALL RIGHTS RESERVED. No part of this work covered by the copyright hereon may be reproduced in any form or by any means—graphic, electronic, or mechanical, including photocopying, recording, taping, Web distribution, or information storage and retrieval systems—without the written permission of the publisher.

For permission to use material from the text or product, contact us by

Tel.   (800) 730-2214
Fax   (800) 730-2215
www.thomsonrights.com

ISBN: 1-4018-1573-1

NOTICE TO THE READER

Publisher does not warrant or guarantee any of the products described herein or perform any independent analysis in connection with any of the product information contained herein. Publisher does not assume, and expressly disclaims, any obligation to obtain and include information other than that provided to it by the manufacturer.

The reader is expressly warned to consider and adopt all safety precautions that might be indicated by the activities herein and to avoid all potential hazards. By following the instructions contained herein, the reader willingly assumes all risks in connection with such instructions.

The publisher makes no representation or warranties of any kind, including but not limited to, the warranties of fitness for particular purpose or merchantability, nor are any such representations implied with respect to the material set forth herein, and the publisher takes no responsibility with respect to such material. The publisher shall not be liable for any special, consequential, or exemplary damages resulting, in whole or part, from the readers' use of, or reliance upon, this material.

Dedication

This book is dedicated to my father and illustrator, Ed Vebell, who not only helped in teaching me how to draw, but also set the example of what a really good drawing is.

table of contents

TABLE OF CONTENTS

V

exploring the basics of drawing

preface

INTENDED AUDIENCE

The notion that you need some special art gene to learn how to draw is not true. Anyone can learn to draw if they have the desire. Having the ability to draw is a way of visually communicating ideas, a necessity for either the commercial or fine artist. *Exploring The Basics of Drawing* explains how to simplify any object, no matter how complex, in order to understand what you see. It helps you then develop the skills needed to accurately translate that to the paper. Combining this knowledge of how to see with the rendering skills developed from this book gives you the confidence and ability to draw anything you want, including the human figure and landscapes. This is a foundation course in drawing for the professional art student or any individual that seriously wants to learn to draw realistically. The manner in which the material is presented is intended for the novice; those with more advanced skills will also be able to benefit.

BACKGROUND OF THIS TEXT

How this book, *Exploring The Basics of Drawing,* came to be began with the need to create an accelerated drawing course that taught the beginning student how to draw realistically. As the instructor and a professional illustrator, I took all that I knew and then simplified it into a logical progression. I began by breaking down how I think, what I see, and how I draw. Each week, building on the material from the previous week, I brought different objects to class for my students to draw, so that they might learn and develop specific skills and concepts. During class, I lectured and did a demonstration of what they were to draw for that session. As I drew, I explained my thoughts and decisions. When I was done, the students were given the opportunity to draw what I had just drawn. As the semester progressed, I watched their drawings improve rapidly, along with their confidence and pride. My students became excited about drawing and they did great work. It was at their suggestion, along with their encouragement that I wrote this book.

It is a limiting notion that an art student need not know how to draw with the technology of today. Using such basic software programs as Photoshop and Illustrator or taking a photograph using a digital camera, one still has to understand how to create the illusion of three dimensions on a two-dimensional surface or field. Without the knowledge of value, lighting, and how reality really looks as a foundation (which is emphasized in this book), one can't create anything new and exciting to bring to the market. In addition to understanding how to see and having developed rendering skills, *Exploring the Basics of Drawing* expands the student's repertoire to truly be creative in any medium.

There are no prerequisites needed to use this book except the desire to learn to draw. The concepts and rendering skills are broken down and explained in simple, easy-to-understand terms and reinforced by the illustrations. The assumption of this book is that most people never have really explored nor understand how they see in the first place—the key to drawing.

TEXTBOOK ORGANIZATION

Exploring The Basics of Drawing is structured as an illustrated step-by-step approach to learning how to draw. This book presents the material to the reader in a simple and logical progression of understanding how to see, seeing how it is done, and then getting an opportunity to practice it. This process develops the eye and hand coordination needed to draw. The cornerstones of the chapters are the illustrated demonstrations at the end. These demonstrations are an opportunity for the reader to see how a drawing is done from start to finish using the material presented in each chapter. To facilitate a more rapid development of the skills, only two media are presented to work in: initially charcoal and graphite. Once the reader has become comfortable with these two media, additional ones are presented. Still life drawing is explored at length until the final chapter, when more complex types of drawing are introduced. This way the reader then can apply all that has been learned to further the learning curve in a variety of subject matter.

Chapter 1 begins by explaining how to set up a comfortable work area including proper lighting. Then it describes which tools are needed and how to use them for charcoal and pencil rendering. It also addresses how to pace yourself through a drawing session and to critique a drawing in progress.

Chapter 2 explains how to create the illusion of three dimensions on a two-dimensional surface. Then it explores how to distinguish light areas from dark areas of an object. It breaks down these areas into smaller areas and defines them. The text introduces and discusses how to use the four geometric shapes that underlie every conceivable form to simplify and render an object realistically. It also shows how to transfer this information to the paper.

Chapter 3 investigates value and how to express a range of values as a value scale of grays. It also shows how to determine the value of a local color. This chapter begins an in-depth look at the first of the four basic shapes: the sphere. It explains how you see it in everyday objects and how to draw its shape and its volume.

Chapter 4 begins with the explanation of linear perspective and its importance for realistic drawing. Then it introduces to how to draw a cube—the second of the basic shapes—in one, two, or multi-point perspective. In addition, it shows how to see a cube as the underlying structure of many objects and then how to render this form in tone.

Chapter 5 explores proportion and how to apply it in drawing a rectangle. It also defines the horizon plane and its importance in realistic drawing. Then it demonstrates how to use shading and contrast to define the form of a rectangle, a variation of the cube.

Chapter 6 describes elliptical perspective and how to draw a freehand ellipse. Then it introduces the cylinder and it explains how to see the underlying structure of the cylinder of an object to simplify its shape. It then demonstrates how to draw the cylinder—the third of the basic shapes.

Chapter 7 explains how to create the illusion of space and how to establish a foreground, middle ground, and background in a drawing. With the introduction of the cone, it shows you how to perceive the underlying conical shape in many everyday objects. It also demonstrates how to draw the cone, the last of the four basic shapes.

Chapter 8 explains the importance of good composition in drawing and describes the basic principles. Then it demonstrates how to use the four basic shapes to simplify any complex object and then draw it.

Chapter 9 looks at the role of drapery and its importance in the composition of a drawing. It shows how to accurately draw the form of a fold and give it the illusion of volume. This chapter shows how to draw a piece of drapery with folds. It also demonstrates how to render a variety of different types of fabric, including colored, patterned, and textured.

Chapter 10 explores how to draw objects with highly reflective surfaces, with the emphasis on metal. It defines the characteristics of such surfaces and explains how to simplify and render the reflections on the surface while rendering the form.

Chapter 11 explores how to draw objects made of transparent material, such as clear and colored glass. It explains the unique properties of glass and how to accurately render the shape, interior and exterior reflections, and any objects seen through the glass. It also demonstrates how to draw liquid—clear or translucent—in the glass object.

Chapter 12 investigates additional media. It explains the difference between dry and wet media. It also describes the materials needed for each new media introduced and how to use them.

Chapter 13 shows the reader how to use everything that has been learned so far to be able to render not only the human figure, but landscapes as well. Seeing and understanding how to draw the basic shapes will help simplify even these complex forms. The material in this chapter explores human proportion, foreshortening and gesture. In landscapes it covers composition, creating the illusion of space and working quickly outdoors while the light is changing.

FEATURES

The following list provides some of the salient features of the text:

- Objectives clearly state the learning goals of the chapter.

- An introduction to the art of drawing realistically covers all the important skills, from learning how to really "see" an object to creating the illusion of volume and space.

- Dedicated chapters teach the specific skills needed to draw glass, metal, and drapery.

- Additional chapters cover the use of such drawing media as conté crayon, pen and ink, and brush and ink, while offering insight into the skills needed to draw the human form and landscapes.

- Illustrated Demonstrations, the heart of the chapters, build upon each other and include detailed instructions to further reinforce drawing skills.

- Review Questions, Things to Remember, and additional assignments reinforce material presented in each chapter.

HOW TO USE THIS TEXT

▶ ## Objectives

Learning Objectives start off each chapter. They describe the competencies readers should achieve upon understanding the chapter material.

▶ ## Illustrated Demonstrations

Illustrated Demonstrations, featured in most of the chapters, build upon each other and include detailed instructions to further reinforce drawing skills.

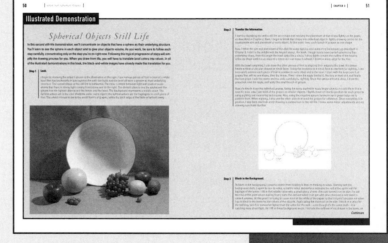

▶ ## Sidebar

Sidebars appear throughout the text, offering additional valuable information on specific topics.

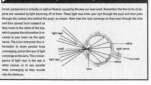

Things to Remember

Things to Remember is a list of the most important topics covered in each chapter.

Review Questions, Projects, and Homework

Review Questions, Projects, and Homework are located at the end of each chapter and allow readers to assess their understanding of the chapter. The Project and Homework sections provide additional exercises intended to reinforce chapter material through practical application.

E.Resource

This guide on CD was developed to assist instructors in planning and implementing their instructional programs. It includes sample syllabi for using this book in either an 11- or 15-week course. It also provides answers to the chapter review questions, additional projects, suggestions for grading, PowerPoint slides highlighting the main topics, and a list of additional resources.

ISBN: 140181574X

about the author

▶ ## Victoria Vebell

Victoria Vebell is a freelance illustrator who has worked in this field for 30 years. Her commissions have been in the areas of publishing, editorial, and advertising art. Her client list includes Bantam Doubleday and Dell, Scholastic, Simon & Schuster, Harlequin, Time-Life Books, Random House, Reader's Digest, and General Foods. She also worked as a partner on one of the largest commissions ever given out, entitled *The History of America in Stamps* doing first day cover cachets for the Postal Commemorative Society. Ms. Vebell works within two distinctly different styles—one realistic and the other stylized. Her work is currently being represented by Art Works Illustration Representatives in New York. She currently is a faculty member at Pratt Institute.

Vicki has always loved to draw and started when she was very young. She began her art education when she was 13 years old with Saturday drawing classes at the Art Student's League in New York. She studied Illustration at Philadelphia College of Art, and graduated in 1974. Vicki is also the daughter of another illustrator, Ed Vebell. He was instrumental in teaching her how to draw. Art has always been a part of her life.

ACKNOWLEDGMENTS

It takes a "village" to make a book. I have many people to thank for their support and effort to get this book to press.

Sincere thanks to Jim Gish, senior acquisitions editor, for first recognizing that there was this book inside of me. Your support and enthusiasm for this project kept the fires burning.

A special thank you goes to Jaimie Wetzel, development editor, for your guidance, support and patience throughout this project. I couldn't have done this without you.

Thank you to my team at Delmar, my heartfelt appreciation goes out to all of you talented, hard-working people: Tom Stover, production editor, Rachel Baker, art and design specialist, and Marissa Maiella, editorial assistant.

A big thank you to Jan Gallagher for reading and editing the manuscript. You made my words and thoughts "sing."

Many thanks to my extremely talented friends and illustrators who contributed their work to this book: Bonnie Johnson, Charlie Gehm and Joel Spector. I am honored to have your work next to mine.

Thanks to my friend and illustrator, Judy York, for your understanding, patience and support throughout all of this.

Thank you Janet Hayes for your support for allowing me to develop this course. You were a great boss and are now a good friend.

Thank you to all of my students; you were the inspiration for this course and for the book.

Delmar Learning and the author would also like to thank the following reviewers for their valuable suggestions and expertise:

Tom Brenner
Visual Communications Department
Katharine Gibbs—Norwalk
Norwalk, Connecticut

Charles Gehm
Art Department
Western Connecticut State University
Danbury, Connecticut

William Livesay
Art Department
Art Institute of Atlanta
Atlanta, Georgia

Heidi Neilson
Visual Communication Department
Katharine Gibbs—New York
New York, New York

Mark O'Grady, Chairperson
AOS/AAS Degree Program
Pratt Institute
New York, New York

Gil Rocha
Art Department
Richland Community College
Decatur, Illinois

Yahn Smith, Chair
Graphic Design Department
The Art Institute of Houston
Houston, Texas

Judith York
Illustrator and Fine Artist
Gaylordsville, Connecticut

Victoria Vebell
2004

QUESTIONS AND FEEDBACK

Delmar Learning and the author welcome your questions and feedback. If you have suggestions that you think others would benefit from, please let us know and we will try to include them in the next edition.

To send us your questions and/or feedback, you can contact the publisher at:

Delmar Learning
Executive Woods
5 Maxwell Drive
Clifton Park, NY 12065
Attn: Graphic Arts Team
800-998-7498

Or the author at:
vvebell@charter.net

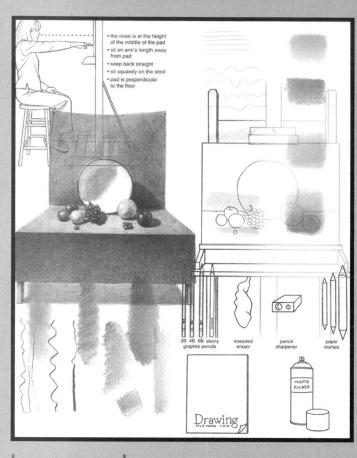

- the nose is at the height of the middle of the pad
- sit an arm's length away from pad
- keep back straight
- sit squarely on the stool
- pad is perpendicular to the floor

2B 4B 6B ebony
graphite pencils

kneaded
eraser

pencil
sharpener

paper
stumps

Drawing
COLD PRESS 11×14

MATTE
FIXATIF

Getting Started

Objectives:

Learn to set up a work area using an easel, drawing table, or board.

Grasp the importance of proper lighting.

Know which tools you need in order to draw in charcoal and in graphite pencil.

Discover how to pace yourself and step back from your work in order to avoid burnout.

Introduction

Anyone can learn to draw. It just takes practice. Learning to draw can be frustrating at times, but, in the end, you can't beat the feeling of pride when you see your first successful drawing. Still-life drawing requires some basic tools, starting with a good, flat work surface and adequate light for both subject and drawing. Then you need your media and some paper. Once you learn a few basic work habits that will help you keep your focus during a long work session, you'll be ready to begin.

THE TOOLS YOU NEED

Every child knows that you can draw with nothing more than a pencil or crayon, a piece of paper, and a flat surface to put the paper on. You need the same basic tools—plus a few extras—for still-life drawing; they're a lot more sophisticated now than when you were in kindergarten.

Drawing Table or Easel?

Many people think that a drawing table is for drawing and an easel is for painting. However, if you are drawing from life, as you will in this book, working at an easel is a better choice. When you work upright at an easel, you can view the still life and your drawing on the same plane. Figure 1-1 shows what you see when you work at an easel when the still life is to one side of your drawing, you have only to move your head slightly in order to compare your drawing to the still life. A drawing table is better suited when you are working from a photograph or other two-dimensional reference because, once again, you can view your drawing and your subject on the same plane.

The first step in working at an easel is learning to sit comfortably, as shown in Figure 1-2. Put the pad of paper on the easel and adjust the tilt of the easel so that the pad is perpendicular to the floor. Don't try to make your easel into a drawing table. When you use the easel in an upright position, your head also remains upright, so that you don't strain your back or neck. Now,

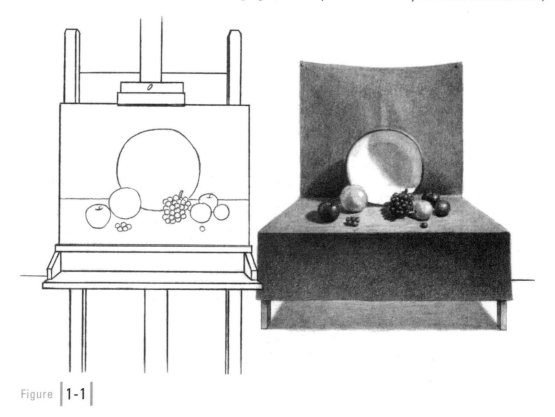

Figure | 1-1 |

sit at arm's length from the easel. You'll be drawing with your arm rather than your wrist, so you need to leave room for your arm to move. Position your chair or stool so that when your arm is outstretched—not bent—your fingertips just touch the drawing pad. Next, position your drawing pad at eye level, again so you can keep your head upright. Adjust the height of the ledge on which the pad sits so that your nose is approximately in the middle of the pad. Now, sit squarely on your stool or chair with your back straight and your feet resting either on the rung of the stool or flat on the floor. Finally, turn the easel so that your subject is immediately to the left or right of the pad. That way you'll be able to see clearly what you are drawing without moving your head more than slightly. This position will keep you comfortable for long periods without fatigue—you'll save your energy for drawing. If you feel awkward at first, don't worry. Once you get used to it, you'll find that sitting at an easel is a natural, comfortable way to work.

If you don't have an easel but do have a drawing table, you can still position it to work from life, as shown in Figure 1-3. Adjust the height of the table and the tilt of the drawing board so that when you sit straight in your chair, all you have to do to switch from viewing the subject to viewing your drawing is raise and lower your head slightly. If your board doesn't have a lip to keep the pad from sliding off, you may not be able to tilt the board very much, and then you may have to move your head more. The less you have to raise and lower your head, the shorter the time you will have to remember information in order to put it on paper. You'll also put less strain on your neck and shoulders. Even though you can't sit at arm's length as you would with an easel, you should still try to draw more with your arm than with your wrist when beginning your drawing. Using your arm in a sweeping motion allows you to draw more of the whole still life. Save the smaller wrist action for the detail work at the end of the drawing.

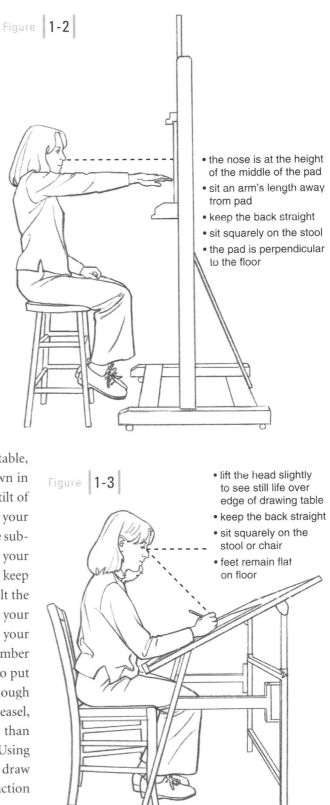

Figure | 1-2 |

- the nose is at the height of the middle of the pad
- sit an arm's length away from pad
- keep the back straight
- sit squarely on the stool
- the pad is perpendicular to the floor

Figure | 1-3 |

- lift the head slightly to see still life over edge of drawing table
- keep the back straight
- sit squarely on the stool or chair
- feet remain flat on floor

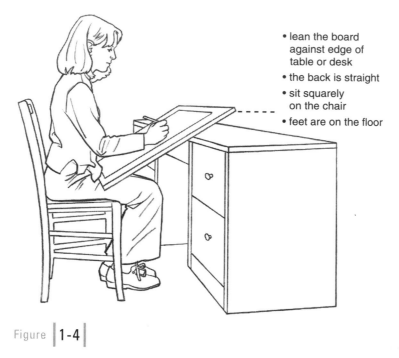

• lean the board against edge of table or desk
• the back is straight
• sit squarely on the chair
• feet are on the floor

Figure | 1-4 |

If you don't have either an easel or a drawing table, you can make an inexpensive work surface. Buy either a piece of 3/4-inch plywood at a lumber store or a drafting board at an art supply store. A drafting board is preferable because it is lighter than plywood and has been sanded smooth. If you buy plywood, you might want to sand the surface. The board should measure about 22 × 30 inches, a bit larger than an 18 × 24-inch newsprint pad. Lean the board on a desk table or the back of another chair and rest the bottom edge of the board in your lap, as shown in Figure 1-4. As when working at a drawing table, position the board so that you can see your subject over the top edge of the board.

Lighting

Adequate light is crucial to the success of your drawing. You need enough light to see both your subject and your drawing. A 60-watt light bulb in a shaded lamp across the room isn't enough. Inadequate light not only causes eye fatigue and strain but also keeps you from really *seeing* what you're drawing—and really *seeing* your subject, as is emphasized throughout this book, is the key to great drawing.

In the classroom, you don't have to worry about the light, which is usually designed to facilitate art work. When working on your own, try to replicate a good classroom lighting situation by putting a strong directional light on the subject (see Chapter 2, "Setting Up a Still Life") and positioning a lamp in your work space so you can see what you're drawing. The direction of the light on your drawing is important—you don't want to work in your own shadow, so place the lamp on the opposite side of your drawing hand. Then adjust the angle of the light over your paper for maximum viewing of your drawing.

Many kinds of lamps will work for drawing, some more expensive than others, depending on their features and quality. The kind of lamp that is the best for doing art work is one that has a long arm with a spring so you can angle the lamp in many different directions, such as the gooseneck lamp shown in Figure 1-5. You can clamp the lamp onto the edge of your table or easel. Such lamps can be purchased at most lighting and department stores; art supply stores also have a variety of this kind of lamp.

Charcoal and Graphite Pencils

For most of the projects in this book, you will use just two media: charcoal for drawing from still life set-ups and graphite pencil for drawing the homework projects. When you begin to learn to draw, using only two media that employ similar techniques enables you to concentrate on learning the concepts of drawing as well as on the techniques of these media.

Charcoal is one of the easiest media to learn because almost any mistake can be fixed and reworked. Charcoal goes on easily and blends readily. You can use the tip of the charcoal to draw lines and then switch to using the side to fill in broad areas of tone quickly, which is important to establishing a sense of volume. You can make subtle gradated areas of tone by blending an area with your finger or paper stump. You can make an area darker simply by adding more charcoal and blending it in. If an area gets too dark, you can easily remove some charcoal with a finger, eraser, stump, or chamois. You can even get back to white paper for highlights, unless an area has been overworked with too much charcoal. Finally, you can use charcoal pencils near the end of your work to fill in details.

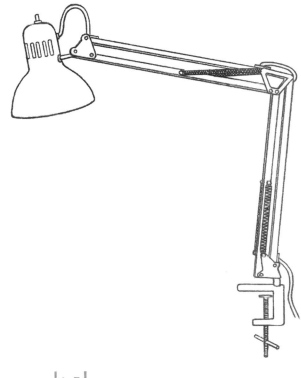

Figure | 1-5 |

Pencil is another easy medium to learn, though it's not really suited for large, tonal still-life drawing. Many people prefer to draw with a pencil at first because it's less messy, and less intimidating, than charcoal. In fact, graphite pencil is better for smaller studies than for large still lifes, unless you have a lot of time for your drawing session. A pencil point is small compared to a 18 × 24-inch piece of paper. In a drawing that size, it takes a lot of pencil work, and a lot of time, to build up the tonal values. You'll use a graphite pencil for the homework projects in this book, which are small studies. In these small studies, you can take your time to build up layers of graphite, creating the subtle gradations of tone that express the volume of an object.

Once you feel comfortable drawing with both charcoal and pencil, you can try doing one of the still life projects in this book using one of the media described in Chapter 12. The concepts of drawing remain the same even though the techniques of using Conté crayon or ink are different from those for charcoal or pencil. When starting out with a new medium, you might have better luck if you don't start to draw right away. Experiment a bit. Draw some lines and circles and do some shading to get to know your medium and its peculiarities. Then, when you sit down to draw, you'll know what to expect—and that will save you some frustration.

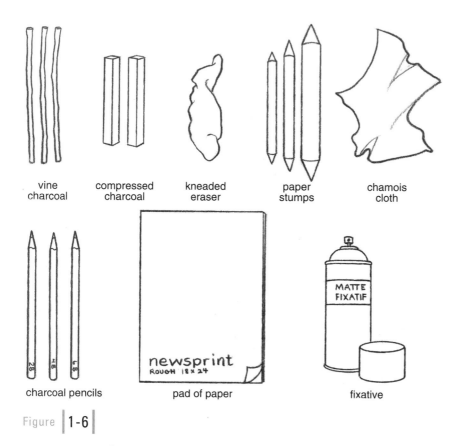

vine
charcoal

compressed
charcoal

kneaded
eraser

paper
stumps

chamois
cloth

charcoal pencils

pad of paper

fixative

Figure | 1-6 |

Drawing with Charcoal

In this book, your still-life drawings from life will be done in charcoal. Figure 1-6 shows the materials you will need:

- Soft vine charcoal

- Compressed charcoal in square sticks

- A kneaded eraser

- A small, a medium, and a large paper stump

- A chamois cloth

- Charcoal pencils, 2B, 4B and 6B

- A 18 × 24-inch newsprint pad with a rough surface

- A can of matte-finish spray fixative

Vine charcoal, which comes in thin sticks, is easy to blend and erase. The best way to hold a stick of vine charcoal is between your first three fingers and your thumb, with the end you're not using pointing downward. In the beginning stages of your drawing, particularly, this position will encourage you to draw with your arm rather than your wrist. When you get to the detail work, you can switch to holding your vine charcoal like a pencil, if you wish, and use wrist action to make smaller strokes. You can get a variety of effects with vine charcoal. The tip makes lines, as shown in Figure 1-7—thick lines, thin lines, or a combination of both depending on how you hold the charcoal and how much pressure you use. The side of a piece of vine charcoal creates a variety of different broad strokes, depending on the size of the piece and the pressure you use, as shown in Figure 1-8.

Compressed charcoal is loose charcoal that has been pressed into a stick. It makes a much darker black than does vine charcoal and can be used alone or blended with vine charcoal. The square sticks are softer than the round ones and work somewhat like pastels. You can make lines with the corner of a square stick and broad strokes with its flat side. Figure 1-9 shows some examples of the strokes you can make with compressed charcoal.

The kneaded eraser is a very versatile tool. You can use it not only to erase, but also to draw the lights in areas that are already dark with charcoal. A kneaded eraser starts off as a square or rectangle; to use it, roll it into a shape like the one shown in Figure 1-6. When the eraser gets soiled with charcoal, knead the charcoal into the eraser until the eraser is clean enough to use again. (Eventually, when the eraser gets very black, you'll have to throw it out.) You can mold the eraser into any shape you like in order to draw light areas. You can even make a point as if it were a pencil to remove charcoal from small areas.

Paper stumps are sticks of rolled or pressed paper that come in different sizes. They are used to blend charcoal into subtle gradated tones. Your fingers may be your first choice of blending tool because they're so handy, but stumps provide additional shapes for blending especially in small areas. When a stump gets soiled with charcoal, it becomes a drawing tool for areas that need to be just a little darker. You can rub a soiled stump on a clean piece of paper to remove some of the charcoal, though it will never return to white. Eventually, when it's too full of charcoal to be useful, you will have to throw it out and buy a new one. Figure 1-10 shows different blending effects that a stump can produce.

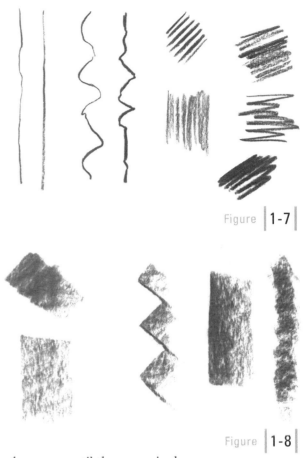

Figure | 1-7 |

Figure | 1-8 |

Figure | 1-9 |

Figure | 1-10 |

Figure | 1-11 |

Figure | 1-12 |

A chamois cloth is another tool for blending and removing charcoal, producing different effects from the ones you'll get from paper stumps or your fingers, as shown in Figure 1-11. Blending with chamois produces very soft areas of gradated tone. You can also use the chamois to remove some charcoal if an area gets too dark. Unlike a kneaded eraser, however, a chamois cannot remove all of the charcoal to bring back the white of the paper.

Charcoal pencils are good for making lines and drawing details. Choose 2B, 4B and 6B pencils, which are soft. The higher the B number, the softer the pencil. After you draw lines with your charcoal pencil, you can soften and blend them with a paper stump. By changing the angle of the pencil, you can get broader strokes for shading small areas. Figure 1-12 shows examples of some of the lines and strokes you can produce with a charcoal pencil.

Rough newsprint paper is excellent for drawing with charcoal. It has just enough texture to hold the charcoal well. In addition, newsprint is inexpensive, so if you make a mistake and want to start over, you don't feel you're wasting your money by throwing out your false start.

Fixative spray is used to adhere the charcoal to the paper permanently. If a charcoal drawing isn't fixed, in time some of the charcoal will fall off or get rubbed away by the back of another piece of paper, and your drawing will look washed out. Always use spray fixative in a well-ventilated area; it's highly flammable and bad for your lungs. Plan on using several light coats. Place your drawing in an upright position. From about 12 inches away from your drawing, spray a light coat of fixative, and then wait a minute or two for it to dry before spraying again. After a couple of light coats, touch your drawing with a clean finger to see if any charcoal comes off. If it does, you need another coat. Go easy; you don't want to laminate your drawing in fixative! If you do, your drawing will eventually turn a dull yellow.

Drawing with Graphite Pencils

The homework projects in this book are small pencil studies based on objects found in your home. The materials you will need are shown in Figure 1-13:

- Graphite pencils: 2B, 4B, 6B, and ebony
- A kneaded eraser
- A pencil sharpener
- Paper stumps
- A pad of white 11 × 14-inch drawing paper with a cold-press surface
- A can of matte-finish spray fixative

2B 4B 6B ebony
graphite pencils

kneaded eraser

pencil sharpener

paper stumps

Graphite pencils are easy to use and not as messy as charcoal, though the techniques are similar to charcoal work. Choosing 2B, 4B, 6B, and ebony pencils gives you a range of tones. As with charcoal pencils, the higher the B number, the softer the lead. The softer the lead, the darker the line or tone. An ebony pencil, being softest, makes the darkest black that graphite can produce. You can start producing a darker line or tone by first applying more pressure to the pencil; then, if

cold press drawing paper
11 x 14 inches

matte fixative

Figure | 1-13 |

you want an even darker line, move to a softer lead. The more graphite you put on the paper, the darker the area will look. Pencils make all different kinds of lines and tones depending on the sharpness of the point, how much pressure you apply, and how you hold the pencil, as shown in Figure 1-14. To make tones, you can stroke the pencil point back and forth in a random pattern, stroke all in one direction, or use a crisscross motion to produce a crosshatch effect. Once you put your tone down on the paper, you can also use a paper stump to blend the graphite for a smooth, tonal effect. If you want to darken an area, add more graphite, switching to a softer lead if necessary, and blend that in with the stump.

Graphite pencils work well on paper that has some surface texture. This kind of surface is called cold press. A paper that has a hot-press surface is very smooth. In order to build up tones using graphite pencils, the graphite needs some surface texture to adhere to. The more texture your paper has, the more texture will appear in your drawing.

Figure | 1-14 |

Each brand of drawing paper has a slightly different texture. You might want to experiment with different kinds of paper to find the right amount of surface texture for the look you want.

When you are done with your drawing, spray it with fixative as with charcoal. Though graphite will not fall off the paper, the drawing can become smeared when touched unless you've sprayed it.

TIPS FOR A SUCCESSFUL DRAWING SESSION

Drawing takes a tremendous amount of mental concentration. If you draw for a long time—say, for three hours—you can become exhausted. If this happens before you finish the drawing, you will have lost your concentration just when you need it most. The final stage, the detail work, requires focusing on small areas all over the entire drawing. If you have worked relentlessly and not taken any breaks, your mind may start to wander, and your tired eyes won't see as well. Your desire to stop drawing will override your desire to complete the drawing. At this point, you have achieved burnout. Your body is telling you to stop working, and you probably should. Unfortunately, if the still-life set-up will be dismantled at the end of a class session, you will be left with an uncompleted drawing. Besides, when you're burned out, drawing isn't fun any more. You can and should take steps to make sure you don't get to the burnout stage.

Trial Run

Now that you have a work area established and have purchased your materials, experiment with them. Each medium has its own peculiarities, and you should know them before you start a drawing. That way you won't get frustrated by asking your medium to do things it can't. Try making different lines and tones with your charcoals. Blend some of these tones with your fingers, stumps, and chamois cloth. Try building up different tones with a pencil by applying different pressure or holding it differently. Add softer leads to see how much darker an area becomes. Then use the kneaded eraser to see how much of each medium you can erase. Have fun! You never know what kind of unique approach you may invent.

Pacing Yourself

Learn to pace yourself. If you were running a race, you wouldn't sprint the entire way—you'd run out of energy before you reached the finish line. The same principle applies to drawing. During a long drawing session, take a break now and then—not a long break, just a short one to give your mind and eyes a rest. Get up and walk around the room to stretch your legs. This stretch will not only increase your circulation and bring fresh blood to your brain, it will also give your eyes a rest. When you sit down again, you will look at the still-life set-up and your drawing with fresh eyes and mind. What you couldn't see before may become clear to you now.

If you are drawing in a classroom, your short break can include a look at how other students are approaching the same still-life set-up. Maybe you have a problem resolving an area, while someone else has already solved the problem in a way that gives you a clue about what to do with your drawing. Maybe you'll see another student handling the medium in a slightly different way than you do and so learn a new technique. You can then incorporate your classmate's technique with yours to create a unique effect.

Stepping Back

While you're drawing, step back every so often to look at your drawing from a distance. It's amazing what you can see from a few feet away that you can't see close up. While drawing, you can focus so closely, so narrowly, that you lose sight of the drawing as a whole—as the saying goes, "you can't see the forest for the trees." Step back, and you can "see the forest." You might find that one area of your drawing looks unfinished compared to another; you've spent too much time rendering the second area and not enough on the first. When you compare your drawing to the still-life set-up, you'll see values more clearly as well, and you'll probably find areas of your drawing that need to get darker or lighter. The value looked dark enough when you were up close to it, but compared to the real object at a distance, you can see that it's not. Stepping back several times during your drawing session will keep you on track—and in the end you'll have a successful drawing.

SUMMARY

You've got the tools for two drawing media, charcoal and graphite pencil. You've learned how important it is to develop good working habits and to protect yourself from burnout. Now you're ready to begin drawing by learning to see the basic shapes inherent in every object.

things to remember

- An easel provides the best angle for drawing from life. A drawing table or board is better suited for working from photographs.

- Good light on your drawing is essential.

- You must learn to pace yourself during a drawing session in order to avoid burnout.

in review

1. What is the advantage of using an easel rather than a drawing table or board when drawing from life?

2. What part of the body should be used for drawing, especially in the initial stages?

3. What kind of lamp is best for illuminating your drawing surface?

4. What are the differences between vine charcoal and compressed charcoal?

5. Name three tools you can use to blend or remove charcoal.

6. What designation indicates the softness of a graphite pencil?

7. Why is it important to take a break from your drawing session every so often?

notes

Objectives:

Create the illusion of three-dimensional space by accurately distinguishing light areas from dark areas.

Define highlights, shadow areas, cast shadows, and reflected light in drawing.

Use the basic shapes that underlie every conceivable form to render any object realistically.

Develop the ability to accurately transfer what you see to paper.

Introduction

Before you can learn to draw, you have to learn to see—to *really* see, to observe your subject carefully and to draw what is there, not what your mind tells you should be there. Since light is what reveals the form of an object, a central part of learning to see is observing the play of light on the subjects you're planning to draw. In this chapter, you'll learn to break any object down to see an underlying structure that consists of only four basic shapes. If you can draw those basic shapes, you can draw anything. Once you've seen the form and structure of the objects you want to draw, you can use several methods, including sighting, to accurately transfer what you see to your drawing paper.

LEARNING TO SEE

The first step in drawing realistically is to learn to see—to see how three-dimensional objects can be transferred to a two-dimensional shape, to see what is really there rather than what you think should be there, to see how the play of light on an object creates its visual form.

Expressing Three Dimensions in Two

We live in a three-dimensional world. All objects, no matter how small or large, have height, width, and depth. However, drawings are created on a two-dimensional, or flat, surface. The piece of paper actually has three dimensions—height, width, and a very narrow depth—but the drawing uses only one surface, which has height and width but no depth. When you look at a drawing or a painting and say, "Everything looks so real!" what you're observing is that the artist has created the *illusion* of three dimensions on a two-dimensional surface. Creating this illusion is one of the goals of good drawing.

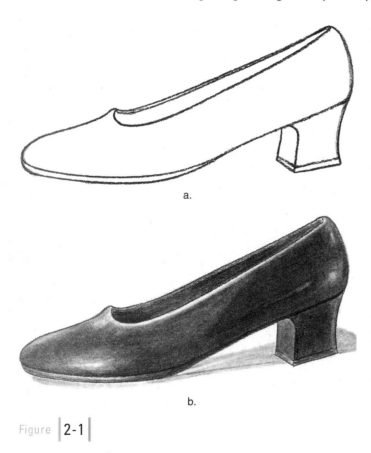

a.

b.

Figure | 2-1 |

To create the illusion of three-dimensional space, artists use shading to create a sense of volume, rather than drawing outlines of objects. Look around you. Do you see lines around the objects you see? You see *edges*, not outlines. In Figure 2-1, which drawing looks more realistic? The line drawing of Figure 2-1a is exactly in the shape of a shoe, but it has no volume. The drawing with shading in Figure 2-1b has volume and therefore looks more like a real shoe. When you start a drawing, you'll often use an outline to represent the edges and define the shape of your objects. This is *sketching*—an interpretation of what you are seeing. There are many beautiful sketches, but they aren't particularly realistic. Outlines flatten the shapes they represent so that they look two dimensional. Shading is what creates the illusion of three-dimensional volume. So at some point in the process of drawing a shape—when you're ready to create the illusion of volume—the line you used to define the shape will have to go.

Figure | 2-2 |

Drawing What You See Versus What You Know

In order to draw realistically, you have to draw what you see and not what you think you see. Think of a familiar object—say, a rolling pin. An image of a rolling pin, probably much like the one in Figure 2-2, appears in your mind's eye: a long, thin cylinder with handles at each end. But what if the rolling pin is turned so that it looks like Figure 2-3? Without really looking at the shape you're seeing, you draw your mind's-eye image—the long, thin cylinder with the handles. But that's not what you are seeing from this angle. The image in your mind is overriding the actual object you are drawing. To draw realistically, you need to forget *what it is* so that you can draw *what you see*. Later in this chapter you'll see how to break down what you see into basic shapes so that you can draw the shapes as you see them.

Understanding Light

Imagine sitting in a room in total darkness. You can't see anything. It's only when you turn on a light that you can see what's in the room. The stronger the light, the better you can see. Light allows you to see the *form* of an object. In order to draw realistically, you draw not only the *shape* of the object but also the *form* of the object as it is revealed by the light falling on it. Rendering the lights and darks you see in an object gives the object its form, creating the illusion of volume.

Figure | 2-3 |

In Figure 2-4, you can clearly see at least three distinct areas: a light area and a darker area on the ball, and a dark ellipse on the surface the ball is sitting on. If you look carefully at the shadow area on the ball, you may also see slightly lighter areas made by reflected light. Creating the illusion of volume depends on accurately distinguishing the degrees of light and dark in these areas.

Light Areas

First, focus your attention on the lightest part of the ball in Figure 2-4. This is called the **light area.** What you are actually seeing is light bouncing off the surface of the object. You

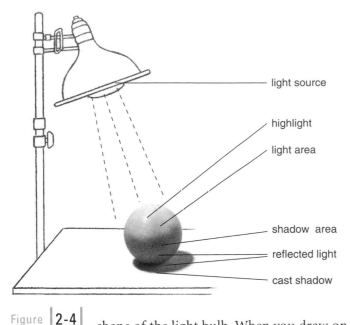

light source

highlight

light area

shadow area

reflected light

cast shadow

Figure | 2-4 |

can't see the rays of light, but you do see the ball's form as it is revealed by the light rays bouncing from its surface. In Figure 2-4, the light is coming from the top left, somewhat behind the object. If you look more closely at the light area on the ball, you'll see some shading and one small area that is completely white. This small white area is the **highlight.** The highlighted part of the object is directly in the path of the light source, a straight line from the center of the light, so that the light rays bounce off that area most strongly. The more reflective or shiny the object's surface, the more distinct the highlight becomes. On very reflective objects, the highlight may even show the shape of the light bulb. When you draw on white paper, the highlight usually remains the white of the paper. Everything that is not in a straight line from the center of the light source—even the rest of the area that the light is falling on—will appear darker than the highlight.

Shadow Areas

Now look at the part of the ball in Figure 2-4 that is darker than the light area. This is called the **shadow area.** It's darker than the light area because it is not in the direct path of the light. If this ball were the Earth, it would be daytime in the light area and nighttime in the dark area. The light area and the shadow area of the ball are as distinct as day and night. However, the shadow area is not solid black; it contains some reflected light, which will be explained in the following section. In order to create the illusion of volume, you must distinguish the light area from the shadow area by shading the shadow area in a darker gray than the light area—and remember, even the light area will have a slight amount of shading to distinguish it from the highlight. If the grays in the light area are too close to the grays in the shadow area, the object will look flat.

Cast Shadows

Turn your attention to the dark ellipse under the ball in Figure 2-4. This is called the **cast shadow,** created by the object on the surface on which it sits. The values in the cast shadow can be as dark as the values of the shadow area, and even darker. The values in the cast shadow are determined by the strength of the light source and by how dark or light the surface on which the shadow is cast. In drawing, you must distinguish the cast shadow from the shadow area of the object just as carefully as you distinguish the light area from the shadow area. Even the cast shadow is not a solid area of tone. The only area in which there is a total absence of light is the area directly under the object; that area is black. This will help separate the shadow area from the cast shadow area. Rendering the cast shadow accurately will anchor the object you're drawing to the surface it sits on. Without a cast shadow, the object will appear to float in space.

Notice that the cast shadow is not exactly the same shape as the object. The ball is round, but its cast shadow is elliptical in shape. Draw the elliptical shape you actually see, not the round shape your mind says you should be seeing. The cast shadow changes in shape and angle with the position of the light source. The higher the light source is in relation to the object, the shorter the shadow will be. The lower the light source, the longer the shadow—just as your own shadow almost disappears under your feet at noon and lengthens as the sun gets lower in the sky toward evening. Always be aware of the height and angle of the light on your object. The sighting techniques discussed later in this chapter will help you draw the shape of the cast shadow accurately.

Reflected Light

If you look again at the shadow area in Figure 2-4, you'll see that it is not all one flat, gray tone. Light from the lamp, the light source, is being reflected off the surface on which the ball rests. This **reflected light** strikes a small part of the shadow area to make it appear slightly lighter than the rest of the shadow. Light rays travel in only one direction—until they hit something, at which point they bounce, acting like another light source. Of course, light from a direct source is more intense than reflected light, just as the light of the sun—a direct source—is more intense than the light of the moon—a reflected source. However, the moon does provide enough light to see by. Though the area that is being lit by the reflected light will never to be as light as the area illuminated by the direct source, it is still lighter than the part that is not receiving reflected light.

SEEING BASIC SHAPES

Part of learning to see—the foundation of realism in drawing—is learning to find the basic shapes inherent in every object, no matter how complex. There are four basic geometric shapes, as shown in Figure 2-5: sphere (Figure 2-5a), cube (Figure 2-5b), cylinder (Figure 2-5c), and cone (Figure 2-5d). Anyone can draw these four shapes. Once you learn to see these four simple shapes in more complicated objects, you can draw anything. Using the basic shapes as the foundation of your drawings will allow you to achieve a realistic look.

Compare the picture of the lamp in Figure 2-6 to the one in Figure 2-7. This complex object is simply a combination of the basic shapes. The shade and the base are cones with the points cut off. The body is a sphere. The stem and the ornament at the top are cylinders. When you can

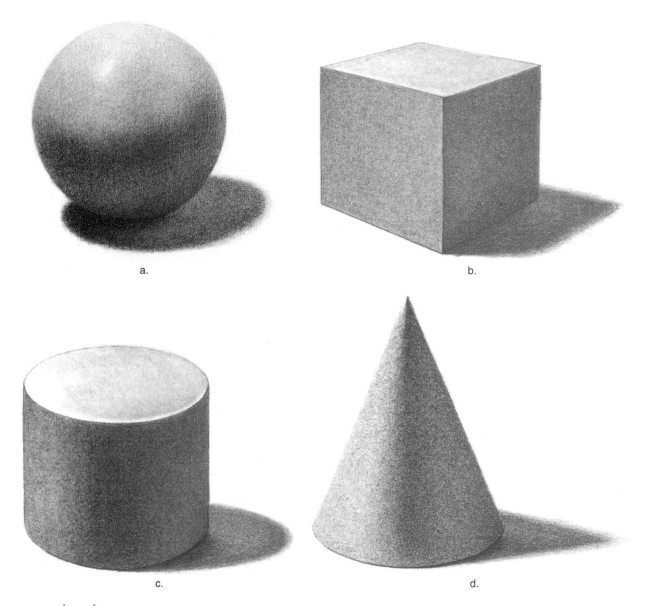

a.

b.

c.

d.

Figure | 2-5 |

see the underlying geometric shapes in an object, the structure of the object begins to seem simpler—and therefore easy to draw.

It's easy to recognize the basic shapes when they present themselves from the angles we're used to, as in Figure 2-5. But the basic shapes look very different when seen from other angles, and you have to be able to recognize a cone or a cylinder when it's seen from above or lying on its side, as in Figure 2-8. You'll concentrate on each of these shapes in turn in this book so that you become familiar with them from all angles. Then you'll be able see the shapes in the objects you want to draw.

Figure |2-6|

Begin your drawing by breaking your subject down into spheres, cubes, cylinders, and cones. Where you see a cube or rectangular object, draw that shape on the paper in the beginning. As the drawing gets closer to completion, keep refining the shapes until finally you have drawn something that looks like what you are seeing. After you are satisfied with the shape of the object in your drawing, you can start shading the object to give it volume, still keeping the underlying basic shape in mind. Finally, you add details to give the object its individual characteristics.

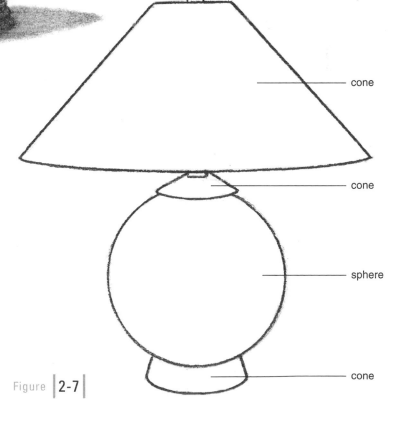

cylinder

cylinder

cone

cone

sphere

cone

Figure |2-7|

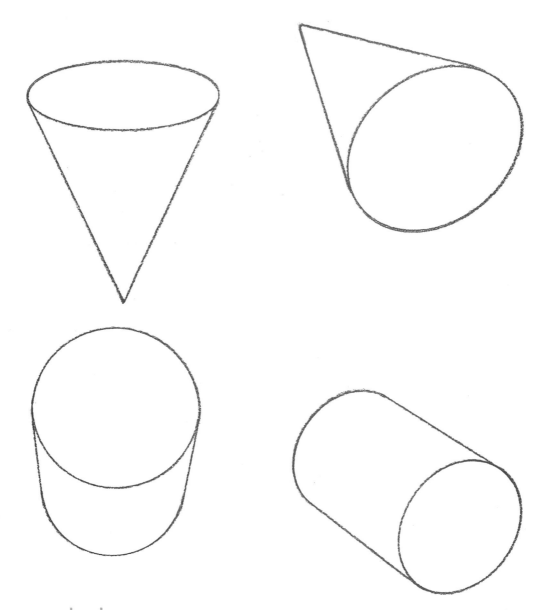

Figure | 2-8 |

TRANSFERRING WHAT YOU SEE TO PAPER

While seeing may be the beginning of drawing, obviously it can't be the end. Until you can transfer what you see to the paper, you won't have a drawing! There's a very specific process to drawing well. If you use these stages in your drawing process, you'll have control over the entire drawing, which means you'll be able to produce a finished work that comes close to achieving the effect you want.

Looking and Planning

When you first plan to draw something, don't start drawing right away! Spend a few minutes studying your subject. Study it as if you never have seen these objects before. Really *see* what they look like. Get familiar with your subject, so that you really understand it. After all, you can't draw something you don't understand! Make mental notes of your observations. They might seem silly to you now, but farther into the drawing when you have lost your direction or your drawing doesn't look like what you're seeing, you can go back to the mental notes you made while everything was still fresh in your mind.

Whether your subject is a single object or a still life, start by asking yourself some questions:

- What object or objects are you drawing? What are the characteristics of that object or objects?
- What direction is the light coming from? How strong or weak is the light?
- Which is the darkest object? Which is the lightest object?
- How dark or light is each individual object in relation to the background?
- What is the darkest and the lightest part of each object?
- What is the largest object and what is the smallest object?
- How much taller is the largest object in reference to the next-tallest object?
- Which objects are taller than they are wide? Which are wider than they are tall?
- What basic shapes do you see in the objects?

Asking these questions will help you understand your subject, which in turn will make your drawing more successful.

Notice the pattern of light and dark created by the light source in the simple still life in Figure 2-9. When there is only one light source, the pattern of light and dark is consistent across all the objects being lit by that source. If the pattern of light and dark changes from object to object in your drawing, the viewer will become confused; it will look as if each object has its own light source. If you can't see the light source, you can still easily determine its direction simply by seeing which sides of the objects are light in value. It's important to keep the light source consistent in your drawing in order to achieve a realistic effect.

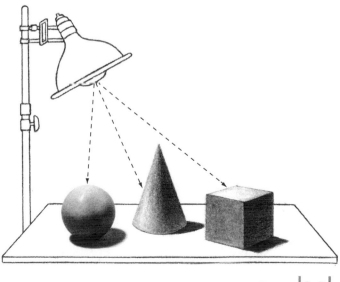

Figure | **2-9** |

Scaling the Image to Fit the Page

Your subject will not usually be exactly the same size as your drawing; so, when you're ready to start transferring what you see to the paper, you have to scale your still life so it will fit on the page. Focus on the whole still life as if it were one object, one total shape. For instance, look at the still life in Figure 2-10. If you see it as one shape, it will look something like Figure 2-11. Now that you have that shape in your mind, try to see it on the paper. Ask yourself, where would this shape look best on the paper? How much space do I want as background around the entire shape? The image should be big enough that it's not dwarfed by background paper, yet small enough that it doesn't looked cramped. Mentally move the image around on the paper until you decide where you want it. Then transfer the shape to the page either by drawing a rough outline as in Figure 2-11 or by making several light marks to show the position, as shown in Figure 2-12. Now you have a starting point from which to begin drawing.

Next, scale the individual object or objects to fit the shape you just made. If there's only one object, you can simply begin drawing it in the shape. If your still life includes several objects, pick a large object either in the center or the extreme left or right. Visualize that object as a shape and see how much space it takes up in the whole still life. You might think in percentages: Does this large object take up, say, 40 percent or 60 percent of the overall space?

Figure | 2-10 |

This will give you an idea of how big that object is in relation to the other objects. Now look at your paper and visualize the object in that same portion of the space you have allotted for the overall still life. Lightly draw a rough outline of that shape. Do the same for each object in the still life, and you'll end up with a set of outlines like the one shown in Figure 2-13. If you find you need to adjust the size or relationship of a shape, simply erase it and redraw it in the correct proportion or relation to the other shapes. Though this method is not an exact science, it will give you a place to start in drawing each object.

Sighting

Most of us have a pretty good eye that is more accurate than we realize. However, when it comes to judging the relative size of two objects or the particular angle at which an object rests, estimating or "eyeballing" is not accurate enough. If you draw the shape of an object correctly but that object is not drawn correctly in relation to the other objects, you have not drawn what you see. **Sighting** is a method for accurately measuring and aligning all the objects of the still life in relation to the other objects and then transferring that information to the paper.

To sight, hold your pencil or piece of charcoal between your thumb and first two fingers so that most of the drawing tool extends either vertically, as in Figure 2-14, or horizontally, as in Figure 2-15. If you are right-handed, close your left eye; if you are left-handed, close your right eye. Always use the same eye to sight with, or else the objects will appear to move and you won't get accurate information. Extend your arm and lock your elbow. Your arm must always remain at the same distance from your eye in order to get consistent measurements. Look past your drawing tool at the object you want to measure. Align the point of the pencil

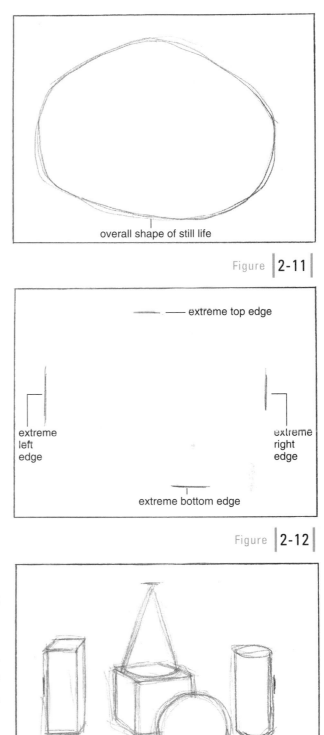

overall shape of still life

Figure | **2-11** |

extreme top edge

extreme left edge

extreme right edge

extreme bottom edge

Figure | **2-12** |

Figure | **2-13** |

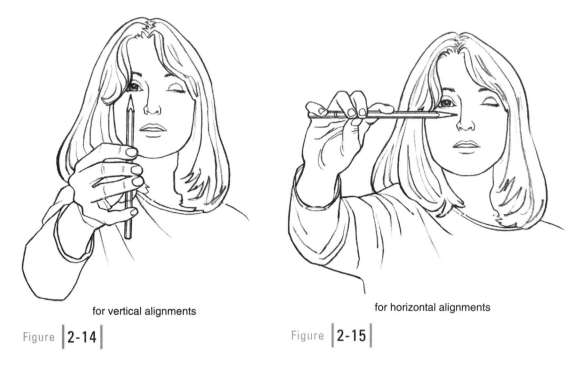

for vertical alignments

Figure | 2-14 |

for horizontal alignments

Figure | 2-15 |

or charcoal at one end of the object, and adjust the position of your thumb on the drawing tool to correspond to the other end of the object, as shown in Figure 2-16.

Now, without moving your thumb, move your arm from the shoulder—keep your elbow locked—to sight another object with your drawing tool. The space between the point of your drawing tool and your thumb lets you compare the size of the new object with that of the old object, as shown in Figure 2-17. Is the new object bigger or smaller than the old one? How much bigger or smaller? The space between the tip of your pencil and your thumb provides a unit of measure for comparison. Using this method consistently ensures that every object in your drawing will be in proper proportion to every other object.

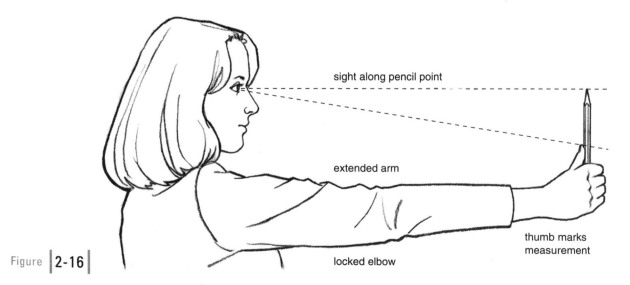

sight along pencil point

extended arm

thumb marks measurement

Figure | 2-16 |

locked elbow

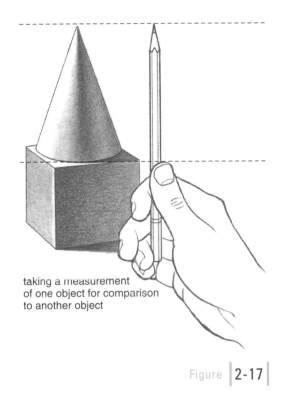

taking a measurement
of one object for comparison
to another object

Figure | 2-17 |

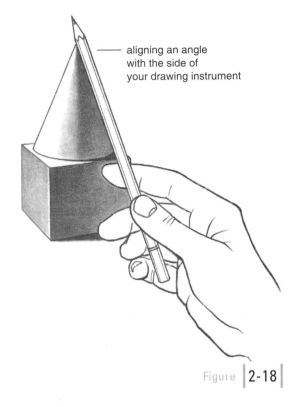

aligning an angle
with the side of
your drawing instrument

Figure | 2-18 |

Sighting can also be used to measure angles. For instance, to measure the angle of the side of the cone in Figure 2-18, extend your arm, close your eye, and align the edge of your drawing tool with the side of the cone. Now, without moving your hand and keeping your elbow locked, move your arm from your shoulder so your hand is in front of your paper. Your drawing tool shows you how to draw the angle of the side of the cone on your paper, as in Figure 2-19. Since the object is a three-dimensional shape, the way to turn it into two dimensions is to flatten your drawing tool against the paper while maintaining the same angle and then draw a line on the paper that represents that side. Repeat this method for the other side of the cone.

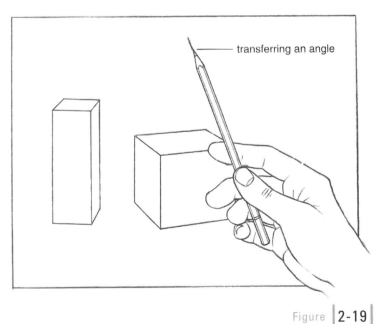

transferring an angle

Figure | 2-19 |

Other means of sighting are shown in Figure 2-20. You can establish the midpoint of an object so that the top half of the object is in proportion to the bottom half. You can use your drawing tool as a carpenter's level or plumb line to establish vertical and horizontal alignments of your

Setting Up a Still Life

In class, still lifes will be set up for you. But you may want to set up your own still lifes at home. First, think about the kinds of things you would like to draw. Choose objects that you like or are interested in, because how you feel about the objects will come across in the drawing. If you don't particularly like the things you're drawing, you might not put the time and effort to make a really good drawing. Besides, drawing is supposed to be fun, and it will be more fun if you draw objects that appeal to you.

Start by looking around your own home. Presumably you like most of the things you own—if not, maybe it's time for some spring cleaning! Choose objects that are simple in shape at first. That carved wooden statue from Hawaii might not be a good choice if you are just learning to draw. It's a complex shape made up of a combination of several of the basic shapes. Be patient: try drawing it when you learn to draw complex objects by studying Chapter 8. Walk around your home looking for the four basic shapes. You'll be surprised to see how many you'll find that would be fun to draw. Your kitchen is full of basic shapes. What about your favorite coffee mug or that one bowl your corn flakes always taste better in? Draw one of those, and then set up a group of objects that have similar basic shapes, such as a bowl, a ball, and an apple. They're completely different from each other, but all have a sphere as the underlying shape. The similarity will help unify your drawing. Later, you might combine this group with a book and a box, which both have cubes as their basic shapes. The contrast of the cubic shapes with the spherical shapes will make the composition of your still life more visually dynamic.

Other good sources for objects to draw are flea markets, thrift stores, and tag sales, where you can find interesting objects for very little money. (If you're like most struggling art students, it's a good idea to set a limit ahead

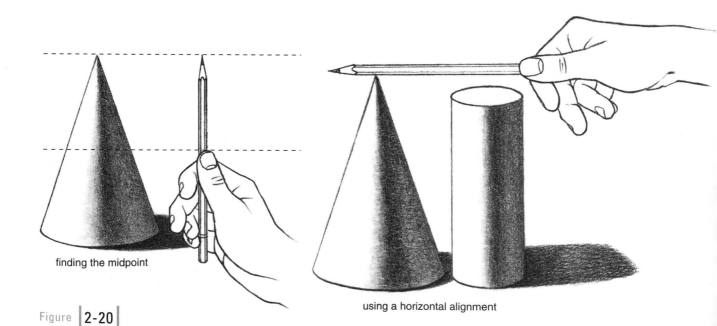

finding the midpoint

using a horizontal alignment

Figure | 2-20 |

of time on how much you will spend.) Walk around looking for objects that appeal to you and are simple in shape. Choose a variety of shapes so that you can mix and match them with the objects from your home. You can do an almost infinite number of still lifes with just a few well-chosen objects.

Your objects will need a background. A wall in front of which you can put a table to hold the still-life objects is a start. Now you want to provide contrast between the objects and the wall and table; the best choice is a plain piece of fabric. If you don't already have some, go to a fabric store and buy a couple of yards of each of two inexpensive, unpatterned fabrics: one light-colored, against which you'll place dark objects, and one dark for the light objects. If you have money left over, buy a third piece of fabric in a middle value so you can contrast your lighter objects and your darker objects in the same still life.

Now, you need a light source to point at the still life (in addition to a light for your drawing, as described in Chapter 1). You want a strong light, at least 75 watts, so that you can clearly see the patterns of light and dark in your subject. The best light source is a photoflood lamp with a reflector shade and a clamp that you can use to attach the lamp to a stand. The stand gives you the flexibility to move the lamp, or raise and lower it, to light any part of the still life. Before you start, check to see where the nearest electrical outlet is in relation to the still life. You may need an extension cord to allow you to move the light so that you can get a variety of lighting effects without worrying if you can reach the outlet. These items are all relatively inexpensive at your local hardware store.

A word of caution: a photoflood lamp gets hot during use. Before you touch it, shut it off and let it cool.

objects and transfer them one at a time to your paper. In the same way, you can establish comparative measurements between your objects.

Learning how to sight properly will take some practice. It may seem awkward at first, but once you get the hang of it, it will become second nature. Once that happens, the results will give you confidence to draw anything.

Focusing on Positive and Negative Space

So far all of our attention has been focused on the objects in the still life—what's called the **positive space,** the actual physical space the objects take up. Now you must also look at the rest of the space, where there aren't any objects—the **negative space,** illustrated in Figure 2-21. You may never have thought about negative space before. Why would you, when what you want to draw is

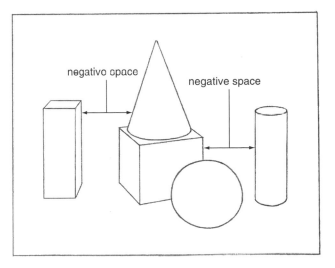

negative space

negative space

Figure **2-21**

the objects themselves? Nevertheless, in drawing, the negative space is valuable information. Though we don't pay attention to it, we do see it. The negative space is as important as the positive space.

Awareness of negative space will make your drawing more accurate. You have to switch your seeing to look at the negative spaces as shapes in their own right. Let's say the objects you've drawn look exactly like the objects in front of you. Now switch your thinking and look at the negative space. Do the spaces *between* the objects in your drawing have exactly the same shape as the spaces between the real objects? If not, the relationships between the objects in your drawing aren't entirely accurate. You might have been so concentrated on the positive space of one object that you didn't notice that it is actually higher or lower, for instance, in the picture plane than you drew it.

Don't wait until all your objects are already drawn to consider the negative space. Look at the positive and the negative space together throughout the drawing process. That will save you from having to erase an object that is drawn perfectly well but isn't correctly positioned in relation to the other objects. The positive space creates the negative space, but both are equally important.

SUMMARY

The first and most important step in learning to draw is learning to see. You'll practice this vital skill throughout this book, refining your ability to discern the basic shapes in any object and to accurately render the play of light and shadow on the objects you draw. The next several chapters will focus on each of the shapes in turn, starting with the sphere. In Chapter 3 you'll also begin to understand how to accurately render the light and dark values you see in your subject.

Illustrated Demonstration

Basic Shapes Still Life

Now it's time to put it all together by actually seeing how I draw a still life. This and all the other demonstrations in this book are presented step by step. Follow each step carefully, referring to the appropriate illustration, so you can understand what you should be seeing and how you should be drawing at each step. When it's time for you to draw a similar kind of still life, use these steps to guide you through to the end. Don't go on to the next step until you have completed in your drawing what I have completed in mine. These steps represent good drawing habits and establish a logical progression that will give you control of your drawing. If you follow these steps in your own drawings, you will know when you are finished—not because you are exhausted and can't do any more, but because you have made a complete statement.

Step 1 | **Look.**

Begin by studying the still life shown below. Make mental notes about everything you see, like this: I see light-colored geometric shapes, sitting on a table, contrasted against a dark cloth for a background. The overall shape of the group of objects is horizontal, so I will turn my pad to the horizontal format. The light source is to the left of

Continues

Illustrated Demonstration

Continued

and above the objects, so all the light areas will be on the left sides of the objects and the shadow areas on the right sides. This light is strong; it creates a distinct contrast between the light areas and shadow areas. The cast shadows are to the right of their objects; the size and angle of the cast shadows indicates that the light is not only high but also directly to the side of the objects. The darkest values are found directly under each object as well as on the wall in the background. The lightest values are the highlights. The ball is the object closest to me, so this is where most of the values will be more extreme. The table line, being farthest from my eye, is where the values will be less extreme.

Step 2 | **Transfer the Information.**

I start by visualizing the entire still life on my page. Where is it going to be on the paper? Looking at the outer edges of the still life, I choose to make four marks representing the outermost edges of the objects in the still life. I make sure to leave room around the edges in case I need to make adjustments later.

Narrowing my focus to each object, I scale each one in my mind to fit in the area I have marked on the paper. Then I sketch lightly and roughly a basic shape for each object for size and positioning in case I need to erase it. I begin with the cone and then the cube because they are mostly in the center of the still life. From there I draw the sphere in front of the cube, then the cylinder to the right and finally the rectangle—using not only the positive space but the negative space as well to double-check the positioning and size of each object. I use the cone as reference to help me draw the other objects in relation to it. I draw in the line of the back edge of the table and use that as another reference point. Once these shapes roughly resemble what I see, I can begin to refine each shape. I start again with the cone. Using all of the sighting and measuring techniques, I draw it by transferring the angles of the edges, and then the curve of the ellipse at the bottom. Once the cone is refined, I then can move to the cube. Again I transfer the angles of the edges, measuring one area for size comparison to another area. I also use horizontal and vertical plumb lines to see where one edge is in relation to another and to the cone. Now, I can accurately draw the sphere in relation to the cube by drawing a freehand circle, trying to make it as round as possible. Continuing to use all the sighting and measuring techniques as before, in addition to the negative space, I draw the cylinder next to the sphere and then the rectangle, all in relation to the cone. I darken my lines to see my objects more clearly because I am more confident that I won't have much to erase any more. I step back and compare my drawing to the actual still life; this is the resulting sketch.

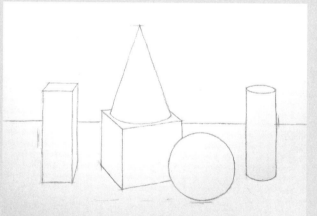

Step 3 | **Block in the Background.**

At this stage, I stop thinking in line and start thinking in tone. Breaking off a 3-inch piece of vine charcoal, I turn it on its side and fill in the background tone. I cover the lines I made for the objects' edges with the tone for the background. Even though the background is a dark cloth, I don't make it the darkest black, value 10 for the wall. (Remember, the darkest value in the still life is in the cast shadow directly under each object.) Nor do I make the same part of cloth on the table as dark in value as the wall; the tabletop is lighter than the wall because it's in the direct path of the light. Vine charcoal won't make a value 10 black. Anyway, I don't worry about making anything too dark at this point. I'll adjust the background later; for now I want only some tone there. Using a paper stump or my fingers, I blend the charcoal. I also don't worry about losing some of the edges because I can always clean them up later with the kneaded eraser. At this stage, I only want to make sure the lines have been blended in with the background. Now my drawing shows white shapes against a dark background.

Step 4 | **Block in the Tones.**

Now I squint my eyes in order to see the shapes of the shadows and cast shadow areas of the objects. Using the side of a small piece of vine charcoal, I quickly fill in the shapes of the shadows for each object. I'm always aware of the direction and pathway of the light. I pay close attention to the shapes of the cast shadows and make sure they all go in the same direction. The cast shadows are somewhat darker than the shadow areas of the objects. Notice how the cast shadow from the rectangle goes up the side of the cube.

Right now my drawing looks pretty messy, as you can see. Messy is good! At this stage the drawing should look loose. It will get more refined as I continue to work on the shapes and add detail. My goal at this stage is to capture a feeling of light and shade in the entire still life.

Continues

Illustrated Demonstration

Continued

Step 5 | **Create Volume.**

The previous two steps focused on the still life as a whole. Now I focus again on each individual object to see the subtle patterns of reflected light and gradations. This is where I start to give each object its three-dimensional quality. I squint to see the different values. In the shadow areas, I darken the areas that are closest to me in each object in order to increase the contrast in value between the light area and the shadow area, which helps make the centers of the curved objects come forward. Now that I've darkened some areas, the shadow area tone I blocked in originally becomes the reflected light in the shadow.

Having created volume in shadow areas, I now turn to the subtle gradations of tone in the light areas. I find the highlights in the objects and don't touch them—they stay the white of the paper. I subtly shade the rest of the light area, making sure that the tones in the light areas remain much lighter than those in the shadow areas.

Next, I darken the background to create a contrast to pull the objects forward from it. I add more charcoal in the cast shadow directly under each object, which anchors the objects firmly on the table. Even though the cast shadows are very dark, I want to make some reflected light so they don't look like black holes. I darken around the edges of those shadows. Then I darken the closest edge of the rectangle and cube to bring those edges forward. Now my drawing looks like this.

Step 6 | **Finish the Drawing.**

For the first time, I pick up the compressed charcoal. I use it sparingly, because it's very easy to overuse it and make the drawing too black. Whenever I add compressed charcoal to the vine charcoal, I blend it in with my finger or a stump. I darken the dark values of each object to pull forward the areas that are closer so they appear to be closest to the viewer's eye. One more time, I darken the cast shadow directly under each object, keeping that as the darkest value in the whole drawing. I decrease the value contrast at the back edge of the table by darkening the top of the table to make it recede. I also darken the wall as well, which will help in pushing my objects forward. Once again, I squint at the still life to see the values accurately and then, if any areas in my drawing look different from the actual still life, I darken with the charcoal or lighten with a kneaded eraser, stump, or chamois. If I have lost any highlights, I use my kneaded eraser to remove any charcoal from those areas.

Finally, I step back from my drawing and compare it to the still life. How does it look? Does something need to be darker, lighter, softer, or sharper? If so, I adjust again. Viewing the drawing and the still life together from a distance gives me a new vantage point from which to judge it. If all is well, as in the accompanying illustration, I am done. I sign my name and spray fixative on my drawing, one light coat at a time, to preserve it.

things to remember

- One of the most important goals in drawing is to create the illusion of three dimensions in a two-dimensional space.

- Draw what you see, not what you think you see.

- There are no outlines in reality, only edges.

- The lightest areas in a still life are the highlights. The darkest areas are in the part of the cast shadow directly under the object.

- Reflected light changes the values of shadow areas and of cast shadows.

- Every object is based on one or more basic shapes. The basic shapes are sphere, cube, cylinder, and cone.

- Look before you draw.

- Always lock your elbow when sighting and when transferring the information to the page.

- Always close the same eye when sighting.

- Negative space is as important as positive space.

in review

1. What is the effect of including outlines around the shapes of objects you draw?

2. How can you create the illusion of volume in a two-dimensional drawing?

3. Which is darker, the lightest tone of the shadow area or the darkest tone in the light area?

4. What makes some parts of the shadow areas lighter than other parts?

5. What are the four basic shapes?

6. What should always be the first step in making a drawing?

7. How can you use the sighting method to determine the relative size of two objects?

8. What is negative space and why is it important?

project

Using vine and compressed charcoal and 18 × 24 newsprint, make a series of quick sketches of individual, everyday objects based on the basic geometric shapes. For spheres, you might choose a ball, a couple of bowls, an egg, and some fruit. Cubic and rectangular objects include books and boxes. For cylinders, you might use a mug, a roll of paper towels, and a rolling pin. Conical objects might include funnels, an ice cream cone (minus the ice cream), and a lampshade or conical flower vase. Each of these objects, except the ball, looks different from different angles, so try setting the objects up in various ways. Keep the light source the same throughout this exercise. Spend fifteen minutes sketching each object. Begin by observing, then draw a quick outline exactly as you see the object. Block in tones for the shadow areas and cast shadows. When fifteen minutes are up, move to another object, perhaps on the same piece of paper. In two hours, you will have eight quick sketches. The most successful ones will be those whose shapes accurately reflect what you were seeing and whose highlights and shadows begin to suggest the illusion of volume.

homework

Set up a still-life drawing area in your own home, coming as close as you can to the suggestions in this chapter on lighting and backgrounds. Line up four objects, one for each of the basic shapes, as described in the previous project. Using your graphite pencils and 11 × 14-inch cold-press paper, make three small drawings of your still life from three different angles or positions, spending about forty minutes on each. Practice positioning the still life as a whole on the page, either by making marks or by drawing an entire shape. Then scale each of the images to fit inside the overall shape and sketch them in. Redefine your shapes by using the sighting and measuring techniques described in this chapter. Then loosely block in tones for the background and the shadow areas. Give each shape some volume—and stop there. Your drawings will look more like sketches than like a completed drawing, as in the previous illustrated demonstration.

notes

Value and Spherical Shapes

3

Objectives:

Understand value and express a range of values as a value scale of grays.

Determine the value of the local colors of the objects in a still life on a value scale.

See the spherical shapes, including partial or modified spheres, in everyday objects.

Draw a reasonably accurate freehand circle.

Draw a spherical shape with the illusion of three-dimensional volume by accurately depicting light and dark areas.

Introduction

In this and the next three chapters, you'll refine your understanding of the basic concepts introduced in Chapter 2: learning to see and basic shapes. You'll learn to see value, the index of light that enables you to translate the colors you see into a black-and-white drawing. When you know how to accurately render the values of lights and shadows, you'll be able to give the objects you draw the illusion of volume. The basic shape for this chapter is the sphere—one of the easiest shapes to draw, and one that forms the underlying structure of a surprising number of real-life objects.

VALUE

When you draw realistically, you are trying to re-create the form that the light on an object reveals to you. Creating the illusion of volume depends on accurately rendering the lights and darks you see. In order to do so, you use the variety of grays available to you in charcoal or pencil to represent the values of the lights and darks of the object.

Understanding Value

Value is an index of light. A **value scale** is a way to calibrate the index—no matter what color the light you see reflected from an object might be—into a range of grays from white to black. Figure 3-1 shows a ten-step value scale of some of the grays you can use to recreate the form of an object. The human eye can distinguish about thirty different variations in value, but, in a drawing, you can only depict ten or so different grays. The more subtle your rendering of the values, the more realistic your drawings will look. An individual gray in the scale is referred to as a **tone.** A **tonal** drawing, like the one shown in Figure 3-2, uses a variety of different values to give the illusion of three-dimensional volume.

The best way to see the values in the objects you draw is to squint while looking at your subject. Squinting eliminates some of the detail so you can concentrate on the relative values of

Figure | 3-1 |

Figure | 3-2 |

the lights and darks. Squint at an object near you. You should see the shapes of the lights and darks—the values. When you can see different values as shapes in their own right, independent of the shape of the object, you'll be able to re-create the forms you see.

Comparing Values

All value is relative. To determine how dark one value really is, you must compare it to another value. It's easy to see the difference when the values are extreme, when, for instance, you compare a brightly lit area to an area in deep shadow. The difference is harder to see when two areas are close in value—but squinting makes it easier. With your eyes wide open, find two areas near you that seem to be similar in value. Now squint at the first area. Keeping that shape and its value in mind, move your squinted eyes quickly to the other area and compare them. You may have to move your eyes back and forth a couple of times, but eventually you're likely to see that one area is slightly darker than the other.

Throughout the drawing process, you should squint from time to time in order to compare values. You need to not only draw each object accurately, but also to draw each object in relation to the other objects and to the background. To do so, you need to establish a guide for reference, your own visual gray scale for the particular subject you're drawing. Start by establishing the lightest and darkest areas of the subject as a whole. For instance, locate the darkest and the lightest values in the still life shown in Figure 3-3. You'll note that the highlight on the ball represents the lightest value and that part of the shadow under the cylinder at the right is the darkest. You've now established the endpoints in your range of values, which makes it easier to figure out the values in between.

Having established the endpoints on your value scale, find the value that represents the midpoint halfway between the two extremes. This will become your middle value. Throughout the drawing, use these three values as reference points, always comparing a given value to one or more of them: Is this value lighter or darker than the midpoint or the endpoint? Constant comparison of the value of the object you're working on at any given point with the other values in the drawing will eliminate a lot of erasing later on. You'll also be able to see your drawing as a whole at a much earlier stage, which gives you the control you need to achieve an accurate rendition of what you are seeing.

Figure | 3-3 |

Values in Charcoal

Now you have to translate the range of values you have established in the subject to the paper, using your drawing medium. The lightest value you see becomes the white of the paper. The darkest value is the darkest tone you can achieve with your drawing medium. With vine charcoal, the darkest value you can achieve is about value 6, the darkness of the sixth square of Figure 3-1. For the time being, use that value as your value 10. Toward the end of the drawing, you'll switch to compressed charcoal in order to expand the range of values in your drawing by adding to the dark end of the scale. Don't, however, introduce compressed charcoal too early in your drawing; its dark values are easy to overuse and difficult to erase. Go as far as you can using only the vine charcoal. Then, when you need to make darker values, add the compressed charcoal *only* in the darkest areas. Use only a little compressed charcoal at a time and blend it into the vine charcoal with your finger or a paper stump. Keep squinting and comparing one area with another until you reach the desired value. That way you can prevent your drawing from becoming too dark.

Translating Local Color into Black and White

Most of the objects you will draw will be in color, but you can't reproduce those colors using a black-and-white medium. In this sense, drawing in charcoal or pencil is like black-and-white photography. What you see in a black-and-white photograph is the objects exactly as they appear, except that their colors, and the colors of the lights and shadows, are translated into a range of values of gray. The principle is the same in charcoal or pencil drawing. You see the values of a color and then create tones that represent those values.

yellow

red

Figure 3-4

All color has value. **Local color** refers to the actual color of an object. For instance, the local color of an apple is red and the local color of a lemon is yellow. Those local colors are translated into values on the gray scale in Figure 3-4. When you look at a colored object, you have to see how dark or light the color is in relation to the other colors. The value of the red is darker than the value of the yellow. Once again, squinting is the best way to determine the value of the local color. Squinting allows you to average out all the lights and shadows to see the value for that color. Then you can compare that value to the range you have established and begin to render that value in relation to the other values in the subject and in your drawing.

When you've determined the overall tone of an object, such as the apple shown in Figure 3-5, start by placing a flat tone over the object to represent the tone that you've established for the color red. Leave white paper to represent the size and placement of the highlight. Don't cover up the highlight with the tone, thinking that you can later use the kneaded eraser to get back to the highlight. Depending on how much charcoal you use for the tone for the local color, you may find that you can't erase to the white of the paper.

If the object you're drawing is light in value like the lemon shown in Figure 3-6, you might not want to put any tone over that object in the beginning. The value is so close to white that it would be easy at this stage to make it too dark. Start instead by establishing a value for the shadow areas, in this case the lower right area of the lemon. Later, when you have more values established, it will be easier to determine the value in the light area.

After you've sketched in the objects in their proper places, as described in Chapter 2, begin the tonal part of your drawing by establishing a flat tone for each object that has a dark local value. Begin by making a tone to represent the value of the local color, minus shading and detail. Then add another darker flat tone to represent a value for the shadow area. For the objects with lighter local values, establish a tone for the shadow area only. This process, called **blocking in,** is illustrated in Figure 3-7. Blocking in the tones of all the objects and the background early on creates the value structure for the entire drawing, so that you can easily see the values of the objects in relation to each other. Not only does this process give you control over your values at an early stage, but it also eliminates working with large areas of white paper. Too much white paper can blind you to the true values of the objects in your drawing, much as the headlights from oncoming cars can blind you while driving at night. In addition, you now have a starting point for your values and will have fewer value decisions to make later on.

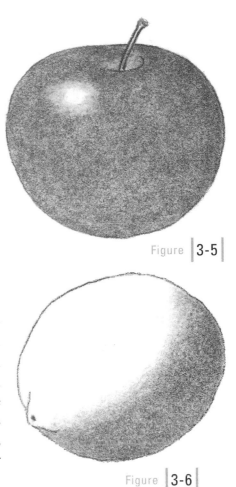

Figure | 3-5 |

Figure | 3-6 |

Once you have blocked in the tones for the local colors of the objects, you can start darkening the values for the shadow areas. For the shadow area, as for the light area, the range of tones for the red apple will be on the darker side of your value scale than the range for the yellow lemon. Squint your eyes again to determine the values for the gradations in the shadow area. With the tone for the local color already established, the only decisions you have to make are for subtle gradations of the values in the light and shadow areas. The result is shown in Figure 3-8.

Figure | 3-7 |

Figure | 3-8 |

Adjusting Value

In a tonal drawing, the more values you draw, the more you will have to adjust them from time to time in order to make them look like what you are seeing. Drawing is like a symphony. All of the instruments have to work in unison to make one overall sound. Your drawing is made up of many elements, all of which have to work together to create a harmonious whole. Periodically step back so that you can see both the drawing and the subject, and look at the values from a distance. Squint while looking at both the drawing and the subject in order to concentrate on the values. Reproducing the values you are seeing in your drawing will make your work look realistic.

You might be so afraid of making a mistake that you hold back and don't make your dark values dark enough. If so, your drawing will look weak and washed out because you haven't accurately recreated the range of values in the subject. Stepping back to squint at the drawing and the subject will help correct this tendency.

SPHERICAL SHAPES

Now we turn to the first of our four basic shapes, the sphere. As you learn to render spherical objects, you'll also practice establishing correct values. Learning to draw a sphere in its simplest form will give you the skills to draw any spherical object. The more you study the simple sphere, the easier it will be for you to recognize spheres in more complex shapes. Then you'll always be able to draw objects based on the sphere so that they have a three-dimensional quality.

Observing the Spherical Form

The sphere is the only shape that is not affected by your eye level; it's the same shape whether you are looking at it straight on or from above or below. A line drawing of a sphere is simply a flat circle. You have to add tone to give the sphere depth and make it look round, as in Figure 3-9. The most obvious example of spherical object is a ball; however, many complex shapes, like the lamp in Figure 3-10, have a sphere as part of their underlying structure. There are also objects, such as the apple and the egg shown in Figure 3-11, that have a

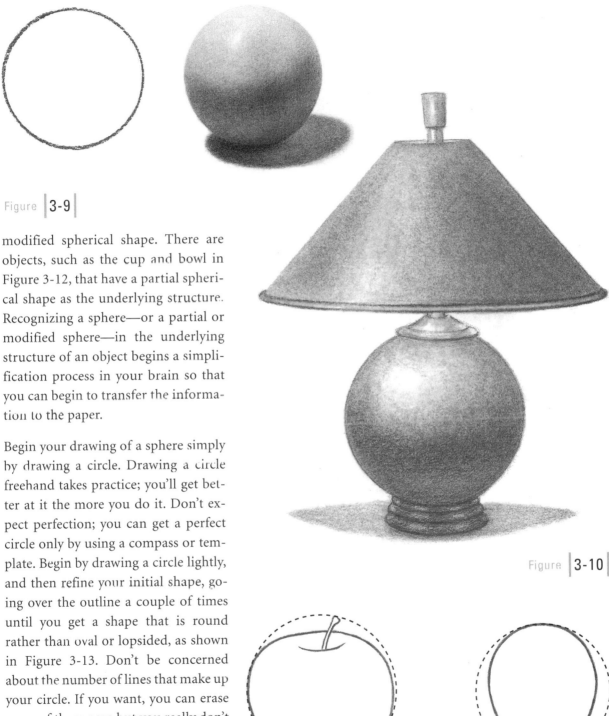

Figure |**3-9**|

modified spherical shape. There are objects, such as the cup and bowl in Figure 3-12, that have a partial spherical shape as the underlying structure. Recognizing a sphere—or a partial or modified sphere—in the underlying structure of an object begins a simplification process in your brain so that you can begin to transfer the information to the paper.

Begin your drawing of a sphere simply by drawing a circle. Drawing a circle freehand takes practice; you'll get better at it the more you do it. Don't expect perfection; you can get a perfect circle only by using a compass or template. Begin by drawing a circle lightly, and then refine your initial shape, going over the outline a couple of times until you get a shape that is round rather than oval or lopsided, as shown in Figure 3-13. Don't be concerned about the number of lines that make up your circle. If you want, you can erase some of them now, but you really don't have to. Later, when you shade the sphere, you can turn some of those lines into shadow, and then erase the lines in the light area.

Figure |**3-10**|

Figure |**3-11**|

Figure │ 3-12 │

Figure │ 3-13 │

Rendering Spherical Objects with Tone

In reality, of course, a sphere is not a flat circle; it has volume and a curved surface. A direct light on a spherical object shows its volume most clearly, as shown in Figure 3-14. Because the surface is curved, the gradations of the tones on the sphere are gradual. The center of the sphere is the part that is closest to the viewer's eye; the edges of the sphere are farthest away. For the sphere to have the illusion of volume in a realistic drawing, it must not have an outline around the edge.

As shown in Figure 3-15, an outline draws the viewer's eye so that the edges come forward rather than appearing to recede, and then it looks as if the edges are closer than the center of the sphere. In Figure 3-16, the outline has been eliminated, so that the part of the sphere closest to the viewer's eye is the part that comes forward. Remember, there are no outlines in the three-dimensional world, only edges.

The shadow area of the sphere is gradated, not flat. As you can see in Figure 3-16, the shadow area has some reflected light in it. Light bouncing off the tabletop illuminates one side of the sphere. Because of this reflected light, the contrast between dark and light values is greatest at the center of the sphere, causing the center to appear to come forward. Thus, accurately depicting the reflected light in the shadow area gives the illusion of volume to the sphere. Note also that the values of the reflected light in the shadow area are darker than all of the values in the light area. The reflected light can help you separate the edge of the sphere from its background by contrast.

Drawing the cast shadow correctly is also important in making the sphere look realistic. The cast shadow of a

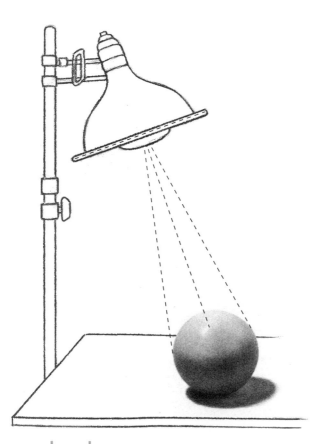

Figure │ 3-14 │

sphere is an ellipse. The height and angle of the light source determine the shape of the shadow. Thinking of the spheres in Figure 3-17 as clock faces, note where the cast shadow begins and ends in relation to the sphere. When the light source is high and from the left, the cast shadow is between 4:00 and 6:30. When the light source is directly above the sphere, the cast shadow almost disappears. When the light source is low and to the right, the shadow is between 5:30 and 8:00.

Now go back to Figure 3-16 to look at the values of the cast shadow. The shadow is not a flat tone. The darkest part of the shadow is directly underneath the sphere, where there is no light. This area is usually very dark, depending on the intensity of the light source. Making this area as dark as possible makes the sphere appear to sit solidly on a surface; otherwise the sphere will appear to float in space. The lightest part of the cast shadow is near the center because reflected light from the shadow area is hitting it.

Figure | **3-15**

SUMMARY

The ability to see and render a range of values is one of the most important parts of realistic drawing. Since light is what reveals the form of an object, depicting the values of an object's local color and of its light and shadowed areas enables you to give depth and substance to your drawing of that object. You also learned in this chapter how to see and draw the first of the four basic shapes, the sphere. Next, you'll tackle cubical objects and use linear perspective to render them realistically.

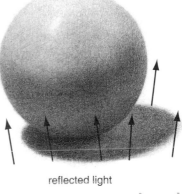

reflected light

Figure | **3-16**

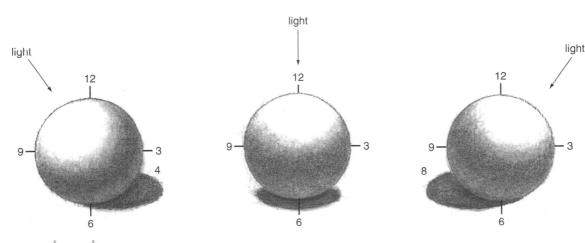

Figure | **3-17**

Illustrated Demonstration

Spherical Objects Still Life

In this second still-life demonstration, we'll concentrate on objects that have a sphere as their underlying structure. You'll learn to see the sphere in each object and to give your objects volume. As you work, be sure to follow each step carefully, concentrating only on the step you're on right now. Following this logical progression of steps will simplify the drawing process for you. When you draw from life, you will have to translate local colors into values. In all of the illustrated demonstrations in this book, the black-and-white images have already made this translation for you.

Step 1 | **Look.**

I begin by studying the subject shown in the illustration at the right. I see various pieces of fruit in front of a white bowl that tips backwards to lean against the wall; the fruits and the bowl all have a sphere as their underlying structure. The overall shape of the still life is horizontal. The clear contrast between light and shadow areas shows that there is strong light coming from above and to the right. The darkest objects are the apples and the grapes and the lightest objects are the lemon and the bowl. The background represents a middle value. The darkest values are in the cast shadows under each object; the lightest values are the highlights on each piece of fruit. The object closest to me is the small bunch of grapes, while the back edge of the table is farthest away.

Step 2 | **Transfer the Information.**

I start by visualizing the entire still life as a shape and marking the placement of that shape lightly on the paper, as described in Chapter 2. Next, I begin to break that shape into individual objects, lightly drawing circles for the approximate size and placement of each object. At this point, I see each bunch of grapes as one shape.

Now I refine the size and placement of the objects using sighting and measuring techniques as described in Chapter 2. I start in the middle with the largest object, the bowl. Though bowls have partial spheres as their underlying shape, from this angle the bowl looks like a circle. I draw lightly around the outline of the bowl to refine its shape until it is as close to a circle as I can make freehand. I draw an inner edge for the trim.

With the bowl completed, I can draw the other pieces of fruit by aligning their edges to the bowl. It's always handy to think of circular shapes as clock faces. Using the numbers on a clock face as markers for sighting, I can accurately position each piece of fruit in relation to each other and to the bowl. I start with the large bunch of grapes first, still as one shape, then the lemon. Then I draw the apple behind it, the lime in front of it, and finally the lone grape. I add the stems and the ends carefully by sighting. Once that group of fruit is done, I draw the grapefruit, next the apple, and lastly the small bunch of grapes.

Now it's time to draw the individual grapes. Using the same method to scale larger objects in a still life to fit in a specific area, now I just think of the grapes as smaller objects. I lightly draw circles for position for each grape by using sighting and measuring techniques. Also, using the negative spaces between each grape helps me to position them. When sighting, I also use the other objects around the grapes for reference. Once everything is in position, I step back and look at my drawing in comparison to the still life. I make some minor adjustments and my drawing now looks like this.

Step 3 | **Block in the Background.**

To block in the background, I need to switch from thinking in lines to thinking in tones. Starting with the background cloth, I squint to see its value: a middle value somewhere between the red of the apple and the highlight of the lemon. I fill in that middle value with a small piece of vine charcoal turned on its side. I'm not worried at this point about making it very dark; the darkest value I can get with vine charcoal is only about a value 6, anyway. At this point I'm trying to cover most of the white of the paper so that it doesn't deceive me when I go to block in the tones for the values of the objects. Again using the charcoal on its side, I block in a value for the tabletop, which is somewhat lighter than the value for the wall—even though it's the same cloth—it is catching more direct light. As I fill in these background areas, I include the outlines of my shapes in the tones, so

Continues

Illustrated Demonstration

Continued

that I can see edges rather than lines. The resulting drawing shows white shapes against background tones, as shown in the illustration below.

Step 4 | **Block in the Tones.**

It's time to block in the tones for the values of the objects, as described earlier in this chapter. I start with all the darkest objects. I squint to see their local values. Starting with the apple on the left, I block in a flat tone with my vine charcoal, leaving a spot of blank paper for the highlight. I do the same for the other apple. Making the tone for the grapes is a little trickier because I have to leave highlight spots on individual grapes. Then I block in another tone for the lime that is just a little lighter than the apple. At every step, I'm squinting to get true values and comparing one value to another. The local value of the grapefruit and the lemon is so light that I don't put down any charcoal on the lighted part of the shapes at all; I block in a tone only for the shadows. I do the same for the shadow on the inside of the bowl since the bowl is white. Then I indicate the shadows on the rest of the objects, carefully noting the shapes of the shadow areas and laying darker tones over the blocked-in tones.

Now I draw the cast shadows by using the sighting techniques. All of the cast shadows appear to the left of their objects because of the angle of the light. Sighting with my charcoal, I align the angles of the cast shadows to their objects and transfer them to the paper. I draw the shape of the shadow, making sure that I'm drawing what I see, not what I think I should see, and that I don't change the angle as I draw. Finally, I determine the values of the cast shadows by squinting at them and comparing them to the rest of the values of the still life, and I block in those tones.

At this stage, my drawing is a loose rendition of the still life. I have achieved a feeling of light and dark and the beginning of a sense of form.

Step 5 | **Create Volume.**

Next, I narrow my focus to the individual objects. I want to give each of them volume by rendering the subtle gradations of tones in each area—light, shadow, cast shadow, and reflected light. Squinting to see not only the value of any given area, but also its shape and its value relative to another area, I increase the range of values in my drawing by darkening cast shadows and the parts of the shadow areas that don't receive reflected light. The shadow areas must be distinct from the light areas, so even the parts that catch reflected light are darker than

the light areas or the highlight. I spend time making each grape round with volume; each now becomes a sphere in its own right with a light area, a shadow area, and a cast shadow. When I have gone as dark as I can with the vine charcoal and still need a darker value, I sparingly add the compressed charcoal. I blend it into the vine charcoal with my fingers or a stump.

I adjust the values around each object for contrast that clearly shows the edges. I darken the value for the wall where it meets the table in order to separate it from the tabletop. Finally, I darken the cast shadow directly under each object to make it sit firmly on the table. The illustration at this stage shows that each object now has a feeling of volume.

Step 6 | **Finish the Drawing.**

To bring my drawing to completion, I continue to squint and compare my drawing to my subject in order to see where I need to darken. I already know that the darkest value in the still life is in the cast shadows, and also in the deepest part of the shadows in the apples and grapes.

Moving around the whole drawing, I make my values lighter and darker until I'm satisfied that my drawing looks like the still life. I reestablish my highlights by shaping my kneaded eraser into a point and removing any charcoal that has overlapped the highlights. In this way, I give my drawing some sparkle by increasing the value range on the light side.

At last I step back from my drawing and look at it as a whole rather than as individual objects. Does anything need adjusting? I compare my drawing to my subject. When I feel that I'm done, as in the illustration at the right, I sign it and spray it with fixative.

things to remember

- Value is an index of light.

- A value scale gives you a way of calibrating grays from white to black in an organized manner.

- In black-and-white drawing, each local color has a value expressed in a particular gray tone.

- The most accurate way to see values without being distracted by detail is to squint your eyes.

- Establish at the beginning which is the lightest value and which is the darkest value in your subject.

- Start the tonal part of a drawing with three values: the white of the paper, the darkest black you can make with your charcoal or pencil, and a middle value between the two.

- Constantly compare your values with each other and with those in your subject.

- A sphere is one of the basic shapes into which the underlying structure of an object can be broken down.

- In a tonal drawing, a sphere is not a flat disk; you create its curved surface by accurately rendering the light and dark areas on the sphere and its cast shadow.

- The closest part of the sphere to the viewer's eye is the center; the edges are farthest away.

- The cast shadow of a sphere is an ellipse.

in review

1. What is the best way to see values accurately?

2. What is meant by "local color?" Give an example.

3. What is the first thing you should do when beginning the tonal stage of drawing?

4. Give two reasons for blocking in tones early in the drawing process.

5. How is the sphere unique among the basic shapes?

6. Describe a method for drawing a circle freehand.

7. What part of a sphere is closest to the viewer's eye?

8. What is the shape of the cast shadow of a sphere?

project

Using fruit or other objects that have a sphere as their underlying basic shape, set up a still life similar to the demonstration in this chapter. Choose objects that have a wide range of values in their local colors, and use a background cloth that has yet another value. Put a good strong light on your subject, such as a photoflood lamp. Following the steps of the demonstration, take three hours to draw a completed still life.

homework

Practice drawing spherical objects in pencil. Begin by finding four objects in your home that have spheres, partial spheres, or modified spheres as their underlying shape. Draw each individually. Use white as the value of the background. Start by seeing the sphere in each object. End by establishing accurate values to give the objects the illusion of roundness and volume.

| Linear Perspective and Cubic Shapes |

4

Objectives:

Understand the concept of linear perspective and explain its importance for realistic drawing.

Create a line drawing of a cube using one-point and two-point perspective.

See cubes in the underlying structures of objects and understand how to draw them.

Use shading and tone to render a realistic drawing of a cubic object.

Introduction

The concept of linear perspective might not be new to you;—you might have noticed that parallel horizontal lines appear to converge as they recede into the distance and that the same object appears larger when it is close to you than it does when far away. You may even have been introduced to a method of perspective drawing that involves a lot of work with straight-edges and T-squares. Good news: There's a much easier way to achieve proper perspective in still-life drawing. In this chapter, you'll learn that method and practice it on the second of the four basic shapes, the cube.

LINEAR PERSPECTIVE

Human beings have the innate ability to perceive spatial depth. When you look at your surroundings, you automatically know which objects are closer to you and which are farther away. We take this ability for granted, but if we didn't have it we wouldn't be able to maneuver without bumping into things! Artists have observed the visual phenomenon of how we perceive spatial depth and have come up with a system called **linear perspective** that allows them to accurately recreate the illusion of spatial depth in cubic objects.

Understanding Linear Perspective

The most basic expression of linear perspective is the way parallel lines like railroad tracks and utility lines appear to converge as they recede to the **horizon line.** You know that the tracks are continuously parallel—otherwise the train would derail—but in drawing, the tracks and utility lines are drawn to converge toward the horizon line as shown in Figure 4-1. The horizon line corresponds to the artist's **eye level.**

You can see how important linear perspective is in drawing by comparing the two drawings in Figure 4-2. Which one looks like a cube? The one on the left is far more realistic because it has the illusion of depth. The drawing on the right doesn't even look like a cube; it's just two squares stacked on top of each other. The top of the cube on the left, by contrast, appears to recede into the distance. Using linear perspective in this way helps you achieve the illusion of volume.

The Eye and Linear Perspective

Linear perspective is actually an optical illusion caused by the way our eyes work. Remember that the forms of objects are revealed by light bouncing off of them. These light rays enter your eye through the pupil and then pass through the convex lens behind the pupil, as shown. Note how the rays converge as they pass through the lens and then spread back outward as they move to the retina of the eye, which passes the information it receives to your brain via the optic nerve. The brain interprets this information to show parallel lines converging, just as the rays of light converge on the lens. This convergence of light rays in the eye is what causes us to see parallel lines converging as they recede into the distance.

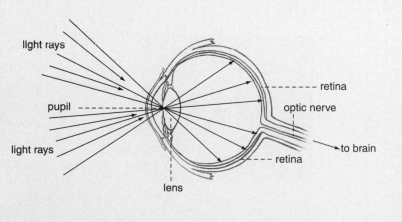

horizon line   eye level

Figure 4-1

Another important aspect of linear perspective is that nearby objects appear larger than objects that are farther away. If you had two apples of the same size, one in your hand and the other across the street, the one in your hand would appear much larger; you'd draw them to look something like Figure 4-3. If you drew the two apples the same size, as

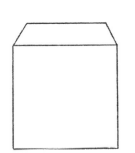

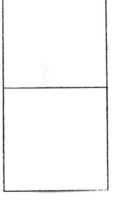

Figure 4-2

Figure 4-3

Figure 4-4

in Figure 4-4, the one across the street would appear to be the size of a house! You've actually already seen this phenomenon in the cubes in Figure 4-2. In linear perspective, the front edge of the cube like the one on the left is closer to you than the back edge, so the front edge looks larger. The problem with the drawing on the right is that the artist drew what he/she *knows* about cubes—that all sides are the same size—rather than what she can *see*, which is that the farther edge looks smaller than the nearer one.

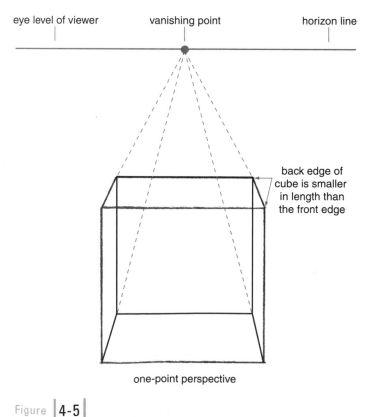

eye level of viewer   vanishing point   horizon line

back edge of cube is smaller in length than the front edge

one-point perspective

Figure 4-5

Linear perspective serves to unify the entire drawing. In Figure 4-1, it's not just the train tracks and utility lines that converge as they approach the horizon, but also the utility poles, both the uprights and the crossbars. The fact that everything converges to the same vanishing point creates the realistic sense that the viewer is looking at the scene from a single point of view. In addition, the lines create a dynamic energy that leads the viewer's eye down the tracks toward the oncoming train. This dynamic creates further unity by giving the viewer a visual pathway to follow.

One-Point Perspective

The simplest version of linear perspective is **one-point perspective,** used when you view an object, such as the cube in Figure 4-5, straight on rather than from an angle. The horizon line, which corresponds to your own eye level, is above the cube. If you extend the sides of the cube, as shown by the dotted lines, they converge at one spot on the horizon line. This spot is called the **vanishing point.** When the lines converge to one vanishing point (rather than two), you have one-point perspective. If you could see a side as well as the face of the cube, you would need to use two-point perspective, discussed in the next section. Note that the front edge of the cube is drawn larger than the back edge because it is closer to the viewer's eye.

Understanding One-Point Perspective

The first step in drawing with linear perspective is to note the level of your eye in relation to the subject, which establishes the horizon line. The shape of an object changes depending on your eye level. In Figure 4-6, you see the same cube from three different eye levels: below, straight on (the eye is exactly parallel to the object), and above. When viewed straight on, the cube appears to be merely a square. As seen from below, you can see that the bottom of the cube and the horizontal lines created by the edges of the sides appear to converge downward toward eye level. As seen from above, you can see the top, and the lines converge upward.

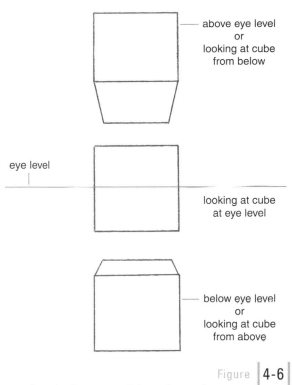

above eye level or looking at cube from below

eye level

looking at cube at eye level

below eye level or looking at cube from above

Figure **4-6**

Now look at the angles created by the corners of the cubes in Figure 4-6. Your mind knows that those are all right angles, and, in fact, that's what you see when you view the cube at eye level; the angles of the front face are right angles. Yet when you view the cube from above or below, the angles of the corners closest to you on the top become more acute, or sharper, while the angles father away become oblique, or wider. The closer your eye level is to being parallel with the object, the more acute or pointed the angles closest to you become; conversely, when you view the cube from far above or below, the closer angles are less acute.

Only the horizontal lines are affected by linear perspective, as long as the cube is lying flat on a surface such as a tabletop. The vertical lines remain straight up and down. The only time the vertical lines appear to converge is when the object is not lying flat or is viewed at an extreme angle from above or below. We'll deal with that situation in the Multi-Point Perspective Section.

Drawing the Cube in One-Point Perspective

If you've encountered perspective drawing before, you've probably been introduced to the method used to establish the high degree of accuracy needed in architectural renderings or drafting. In this method, you start by drawing a line, using a straight-edge, to represent the horizon line. Next you make a mark on the horizon line to represent the vanishing point, which you establish by determining the angles of the horizontal lines. Then, using a straight-edge, you

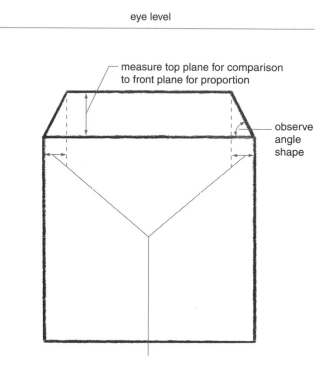

eye level

measure top plane for comparison
to front plane for proportion

observe
angle
shape

determine space difference
between the front and back corners
by using vertical plumb lines

Figure **4-7**

line up every horizontal line between its beginning point and the vanishing point. Though this is the traditional way most artists learn perspective drawing, it's labor intensive. Still-life drawing doesn't require that level of accuracy. Here's an easier way to draw a cube in one-point perspective, using your observation and sighting techniques rather than relying on straight-edges and T-squares.

As always, start by observing the cube closely and making notes of your observations. Most important, where is your eye level in relation to the cube? Bring your hand up to the level of your eyes as if you were going to salute someone, keeping your hand parallel to your eyes. Then extend your hand outward so you can see your hand and the cube at the same time. This shows your eye level in relation to the cube, as marked in Figure 4-7. In this case, your eye is only slightly above the cube. As you continue to observe the cube, you note that, because your eye level is close to the cube, the angles close to you are acute and pointed and the space between the back edge and the front edge is small. You can determine the shape of the top of the cube by sighting with your drawing instrument held vertically. Align the charcoal or pencil with one of the back corners and observe where it meets the nearer top edge. See the difference in the space between the back corners and the front corners. Now you'll be able to draw the cube accurately without having to draw all of those perspective lines.

First, draw a square for the front of the cube. Determine the angles of the horizontal sides of the cube by extending your arm and aligning your drawing instrument along the edge from the front to the back corner, first for the right side and then for the left. Transfer those angles to the top-front corners of your square. Sight with your drawing instrument and measure with your thumb to determine how far the back edge is from the front edge; make a mark for that distance on your paper, and then draw a line through it to complete the back of the cube.

You can check to see if you've accurately captured the cube. First, make sure that the front edge is, in fact, larger than the back edge! Next, squint and compare the overall shape of your drawing with that of the cube. Now is the time for fine-tuning if necessary. Use your drawing instrument to sight along a vertical plumb line from the back corners to the front-top line and draw marks where the plumb line intersects the front edge. Compare those spaces and adjust if necessary. Check the distance of the back edge from the front. Now the top of your cube should look like the one you're seeing.

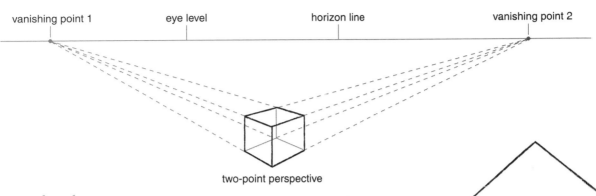

two-point perspective

Figure | 4-8 |

Two-Point Perspective

When you see a cubic object from an angle, like the cube in Figure 4-8, you must draw it in **two-point perspective.** This is, after all, a more common situation than is sitting squarely in front of the object you're drawing. You see two sides, and therefore you have two vanishing points. The horizontal lines on one side of the cube converge to one vanishing point and those on the other side to the other vanishing point. In Figure 4-9, you can see what is likely to happen when you try to draw a cube seen at an angle without using two-point perspective. The cube in Figure 4-9a is accurately rendered to give the illusion of depth, but the artist tried to begin the cube in Figure 4-9b with a square for the top of the cube—which is not what you see from this angle. Two-point perspective is a little more complex than one-point perspective, but the goal is the same: to create the illusion of depth based on the visual phenomenon of linear perspective.

Understanding Two-Point Perspective

As with one-point perspective, your eye level determines the horizon line of a drawing in two-point perspective. In Figure 4-10, you can see how the same cube changes when seen from below, from exactly level with the cube, and from above. The farther above the cube your eye level is, the more of the top of the cube you will see and the less acute the left and right angles will be.

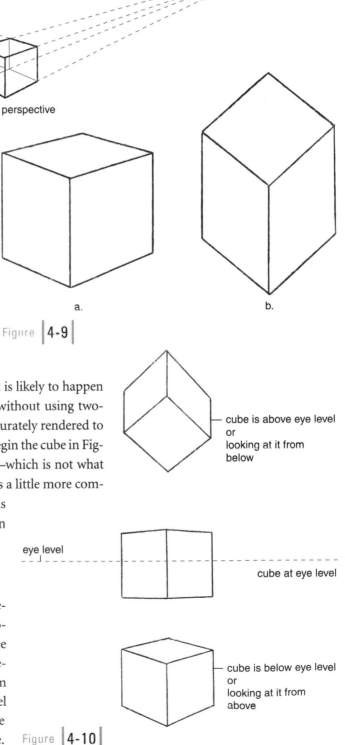

a.   b.

Figure | 4-9 |

cube is above eye level
or
looking at it from below

eye level

cube at eye level

cube is below eye level
or
looking at it from above

Figure | 4-10 |

eye level

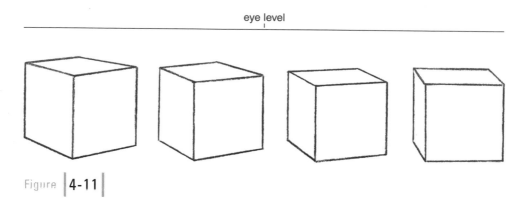

Figure | **4-11** |

The shape of the cube also changes as your angle rotates. Figure 4-11 shows the same cube, viewed from the same eye level, as it is rotated. As the cube is turned, you see more of one side and less of the others. Though you know that the sides are all the same size in reality, you want to draw what you see. You can use your sighting techniques to compare the size of the apparently smaller side to that of the larger one.

Drawing the Cube in Two-Point Perspective

If you can see two sides of a cube—three, counting the top or bottom—you need to draw it in two-point perspective. Start, as usual, by observing. Establish your eye level as previously described for one-point perspective. In Figure 4-12, your eye level is above the cube, but not far above, because you see the sides as larger than the top. Now observe the sides. Because

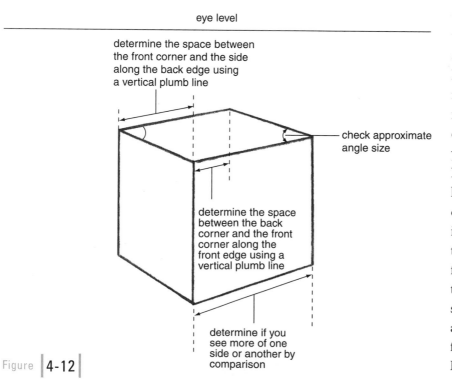

eye level

determine the space between the front corner and the side along the back edge using a vertical plumb line

check approximate angle size

determine the space between the back corner and the front corner along the front edge using a vertical plumb line

determine if you see more of one side or another by comparison

you're viewing the cube from the right, you see more of the right side than of the left side. Compare the size of the left side with that of the right to find that the left side is about two-thirds the size of the right side. Now turn your attention to the top. Note that the angles of the left and right corners are quite acute because the top is close to your eye level. Extend a vertical plumb line from the backmost corner to the top-right-front edge to see that it intersects the edge about one-third of the way from the frontmost corner. Extend a plumb line up-

Figure | **4-12** |

wards from the frontmost corner, and you'll find that it intersects the back edge also about one-third of the way across.

Having made these observations, you're ready to start drawing. This time it's not as easy as drawing a square for one side; you don't see any perfect squares. Instead, draw a vertical line to represent the corner closest to you. Align your drawing tool with the front-top-right edge and draw a line for that angle starting from the vertical line. Next, determine how big your cube will be by drawing a vertical line for the right edge, parallel to the first vertical line. For the bottom-right edge, repeat the procedure you used for the top right. Remember that the front-vertical edge is going to be larger than the back ones, even if it is only slightly larger. Then turn to the left side and establish the top and bottom angles by aligning with your drawing instrument. In Figure 4-12, your observation showed that the left side is two-thirds the size of the right side, so draw another vertical line at that distance to represent the back edge.

Moving to the top of the cube, align your drawing instrument with the back-right and back-left edges and transfer those angles to your paper. Carefully compare the top shape you've just drawn to that of your subject. Drop a vertical plumb line from the backmost corner to find out if it meets the front edge one quarter of the way from the front corner, as in Figure 4-12; adjust if necessary, and then repeat from the front corner toward the back-left edge. When all of these measurements check out, the top of your cube will look like the shape you are seeing. The measurements will, of course, change depending on the angle from which you are viewing a given cube.

Multi-Point Perspective

There is one more kind of linear perspective you should know about: **multi-point perspective,** which has three or more vanishing points. In addition to the two vanishing points for the horizontal lines of the two sides of an object, a third vanishing point is added above or below the horizon line so that *vertical* parallel lines can also appear to converge. You see this perspective, for instance, when looking down from a city skyscraper, as in Figure 4-13—when your subject is extremely tall. Not only do the horizontal lines converge on two vanishing points on the horizon line, the vertical lines also appear to converge to another vanishing point below the horizon line.

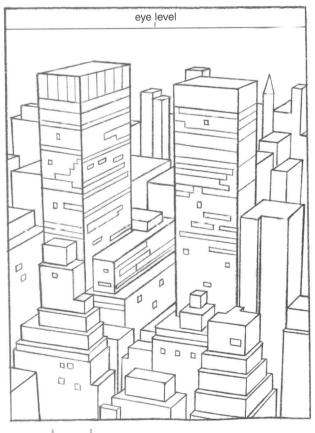

Figure | **4-13** |

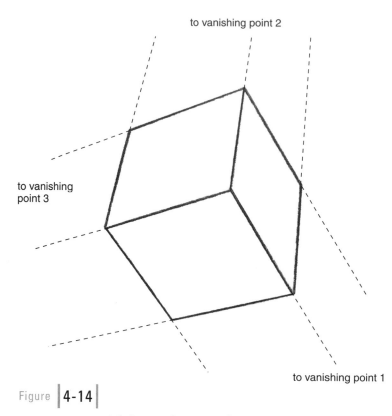

to vanishing point 2

to vanishing point 3

to vanishing point 1

Figure | 4-14 |

You need multi-point perspective in still-life drawing when a cubical object is not lying flat on a surface and you're viewing it from far above or below, as in Figure 4-14. The vertical lines, when extended, converge to a third vanishing point. The more extreme your viewing angle, the more the vertical lines converge. You might need this kind of perspective in still-life drawing if you view your subject from the floor or from a ladder. The techniques remain the same as with two-point perspective, but you have to do a lot more sighting and checking to make sure you render the object as you see it.

Time and practice will make perspective drawing come more easily. Combine your knowledge of the theory of linear perspective with observation and sighting, and you can draw any cubical object exactly as you see it. Remember that you should always check what you have drawn against what you see. If your subject includes several cubic shapes, check each of them carefully against the others to make sure that they all look like they're seen from the same eye level; otherwise they won't look as if they belong together. You may see cubes of various sizes, and they may be rotated so that their angles vary from one cube to another, but you always see the objects in one still-life set-up from the same eye level.

CUBIC SHAPES

The cube is the second of the four basic geometric shapes. The cube is more complicated to draw than the sphere because, unlike a sphere, a cube appears to change its shape as your eye level and angle of view change. That's why an understanding of linear perspective is important in drawing cubic shapes. The most obvious example of a cubic shape is a box with sides all the same size, like the tissue box in Figure 4-15. In fact, boxes with sides that are not all the same size—rectangular objects—are also considered cubes in terms of the four geometric shapes, but we'll deal with rectangular shapes in the next chapter, in which you will also learn about proportion.

The cubes you've seen so far in this chapter have been drawn with line and proper perspective, which gives some impression of volume. However, it's the addition of tone that really gives the

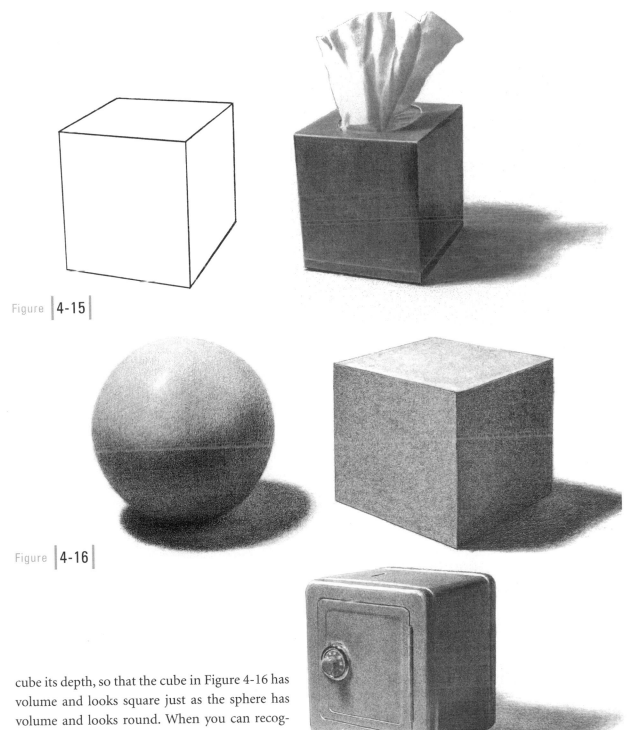

Figure | 4-15 |

Figure | 4-16 |

cube its depth, so that the cube in Figure 4-16 has volume and looks square just as the sphere has volume and looks round. When you can recognize the underlying cubic shape of an object, such as the bank in Figure 4-17, you'll be able to draw that object with ease using either one-point or two-point perspective. After you modify your line

Figure | 4-17 |

drawing to ensure that it matches what you are seeing, you shade it to give it volume and lastly add details such as the combination lock on the bank. If you follow this procedure, your cubic objects will always look realistic.

Observing the Cubic Form

A cube is made up of six flat sides, all of which have the same dimensions. However, as noted, those sides do not look as if they are all the same, depending on the angle from which you view the cube. As you can see in Figure 4-18, placing a direct source of light on a cube clearly defines its volume by revealing the light and shadow areas. The edges of the cube are defined not by lines—remember, there are no out lines in reality—but by the contrast between the light and dark values of the sides. The greater the contrast between the values, the more the edges will appear to come forward; the lower the contrast, the more the edges will appear to recede.

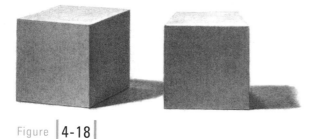

Figure | 4-18 |

The side of the cube that is in the direct path of the light is the light area. As with the sphere, the light area is usually not a flat tone but shows some gradation. The highlight falls on the edge that is in a straight line from the center of light source. When you can see two sides, as in the cube on the left in Figure 4-18, the side closer to the light source, though it is shadowed, is lighter than the side farther from the light source. The contrast in value between the light area and the shadow areas makes the edges between them appear to come forward in the picture plane. The more contrast between the edges, the sharper the edges will appear to be and the more your cube will look square.

If you look closely at the cubes in Figure 4-18, you can see the reflected light in the shadow areas. This increases the contrast between the light area on the top and the shadow areas on the side, further defining the edges to make them look sharp and crisp and giving volume to the cube. The frontmost corner of the left-hand cube, which is closest to the viewer's eye, comes forward because of the contrast in values as well as the perspective lines.

The cast shadow of a cube, as of a sphere, is gradated rather than flat in tone. The darkest part of the shadow is directly under the cube; the rest of the cast shadow receives some reflected light. Making that darkest area as dark as you can helps anchor the cube to the surface it rests on. As with the sphere, the range of values in the cast shadow is as dark as or darker than the values in the shadow area, depending on the local value of the surface on which the cube sits and on the strength of the light source.

The shape of the cast shadow is determined by the position of the light source. Just as the cast shadow of a sphere is not a circle but an ellipse, so the edges of the cast shadow may not follow the angles of the horizontal edges of the cube. Remember to draw what you see and not what you think you should be seeing. As with the sphere, you must use your observations and sighting techniques to enable you to draw the cast shadow accurately.

A cube drawn in perspective actually has two cast shadows. Besides the large obvious one under one side, there's also a smaller one that appears as a thin dark line under the other side, which is also in shadow. In order to ensure that your cube sits firmly on its surface, you have to draw both shadows, including the one you can barely see. Otherwise, one side will appear to be anchored to the surface while the other appears to float.

Drawing Cubic Objects

When you have determined that the basic shape of an object you want to draw is a cube, start by observing where your eye level is in relation to the cube, and then figure out whether you're seeing the cube in one-point or two-point perspective by noting how many sides you can see. Once you've done that, follow the procedure previously outlined for either one-point or two-point perspective to achieve an accurate line drawing. Then observe how the light reveals the shape of the form and render the tones to give the cube its volume. Be sure to establish clear contrast between the edges that are closest to the viewer's eye in order to bring them forward.

SUMMARY

Linear perspective is crucial to establishing a sense of realism in objects that have straight edges and sides. Your eye level establishes the horizon line to which all of the lines in your drawing appear to recede. When you see only one side plus the top or bottom of a cubic object, use one-point perspective; when you see two sides, use two-point perspective. In drawing a variation of the cube, rectangular objects, in the next chapter, you'll use your knowledge of perspective and add a sense of proportion to render such objects realistically.

Illustrated Demonstration

Cubic Objects Still Life

Now try using your understandings of linear perspective and of the cubic form to see how to draw a still life of cubic objects. You should be familiar with the procedure by now; the steps remain the same though the objects have changed.

Step 1 | **Look.**

As always, I begin by studying my subject. I see a variety of box-like objects, all of which have a cube as their underlying shape, sitting at various angles on a table. Since I can see the top of each cube, I know that my eye level is above the still life. The light is strong, originating from above and to the right. The background cloth is quite dark in value. The darkest objects I see are the tissue box and the bucket with the handle. The lightest objects are the dice and the tissue coming out of the box. The darkest values are in the cast shadows below and behind the objects; the lightest values are the highlights on the tissue and on the dice. The closest object is the tissue box and the farthest is the bucket with the handle. Since these are cubic objects, I'm interested in the perspective I need to use to draw them. All of the objects except the tissue box are in two-point perspective, because I can see two sides. The tissue box is in one-point perspective.

Step 2 | **Transfer the Information.**

I begin by making four marks on my paper for the shape of the still life. Then I scale down each object to fit into that area by sketching in simple cubic shapes, indicating each object's approximate size and placement. Using my knowledge of linear perspective and sighting and measuring techniques, I then will redefine each shape as I see it.

I start with the bank. Once the outside shape is accurate, I draw in the details, the door, the lock handle, and all of the other ridges. Using the bank as my reference object, I draw all of the other objects in relation to this one. Next is the tissue box. To determine how far apart they are, I measure the negative space between them. Using the same method as to draw the bank, I repeat the steps for the tissue box, even though it is in one-point perspective. To draw the tissue, I transfer each angle by sighting, then modify it. From there I draw the bucket with the handle, and it is in two-point perspective. Notice that the sides taper downward. To draw the top of the lid, first I draw it as if it were flat. Then I draw the four cylinders by sighting and measuring them using the rest of the bucket as

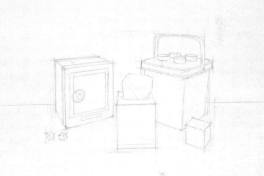

reference. Following is the game cube in front of the bucket, and finally the dice, all in two-point perspective. They are furthest away from my eye level and I see more of their top planes than the top planes of the bucket and bank. They are drawn in, with proper relation to the other objects as well. Notice that I haven't drawn in the dots or lines yet. That is detail and I will add it later, once the volume has been created for these objects. I draw in the line for the back edge of the table. When all of my objects are drawn correctly, in relation to each other, that line will intersect each object as I see it. Then I step back and compare what I have drawn to the still life. The result is the line drawing shown at the right.

Step 3 | **Block in the Background.**

From here on, I think only in tone. Squinting to determine the values, I fill in a darker tone behind the objects in the background and a lighter tone for the tabletop, bringing the tones right up to the lines that indicate the edges of my objects. I blend the uneven strokes of charcoal with my fingers, and use a paper stump to blend the edge lines into the background. Now I have white shapes surrounded by two values of charcoal, as shown.

Continues

Illustrated Demonstration

Continued

Step 4 | **Block in the Tones.**

From my observations, I already know which are the darkest and lightest objects. I start by squinting to see the local values of the darker objects and then block-in flat tones. I leave the top of the tissue box and the bucket white for now. The game cube is unusual in that each face is a different color, which means I block in two different values for the sides and leave the top white for now. For the dice, I block in a tone for the shadow areas only.

Now that I've established flat tones for the values of darker objects, I go back and add darker tones for the shadow areas of each object, constantly squinting to compare values from one area to another. I then draw the cast shadows in relation to their objects. I align the angles to make sure I draw what I see rather than what I think should be there, and squint to determine the values. Now my still life, as shown, is starting to take shape.

Step 5 | **Create Volume.**

For the time being I am still using only vine charcoal; I refine the shading on each object individually. I squint to focus on subtle gradations in value, making sure to keep the range of values in light areas, shadow areas, and cast shadows distinct from each other. I darken areas near edges in order to make the square corners emerge. I darken the cast shadows directly under the object, remembering to include the line for the second, barely noticeable, cast shadow under each cubic object. I also darken behind the objects and tabletop to not only pull my objects forward, but also to allow me to make a greater range of values in creating the volume. This illustration shows that the objects are beginning to look more realistic.

Step 6 | **Finish the Drawing.**

I add compressed charcoal to the darker areas of my drawing, always keeping in mind the areas that I identified as the darkest. Squinting as needed, I adjust values, some lighter and some darker, and reestablish highlights with my kneaded eraser so that they remain the white of the original paper. When my drawing looks like what I see, I add details: the lines on the game cube, the dots on the dice. For the numbers on the bank, I'm going to indicate them by a white line. This area is too small to cleanly draw in each number. I use my kneaded eraser, molded to a point, and make a line for each number. I darken the wall and the tabletop around the edges. This creates a feeling of a spotlight on just the objects and pulls your attention there. I step back to make sure my drawing really looks like my subject, and adjust if necessary. I sign it, but it's hardly visible, and then I give it several light coats of fixative.

things to remember

- Linear perspective is used in drawing to capture the visual phenomenon in which parallel lines appear to converge as they recede into the distance.

- Linear perspective also establishes that nearby objects look larger than objects that are farther away.

- Your eye level establishes the horizon line toward which parallel horizontal lines appear to recede.

- In one-point perspective, horizontal lines appear to converge at one point on the horizon line. In two-point perspective, they converge at two points. In multi-point perspective, vertical lines also appear to converge on a third point.

- Use one-point perspective when you can see one side (the front) as well as the top or bottom of a cube; use two-point perspective when you can see two sides plus the top or bottom.

- If you know the theory of linear perspective, you can draw a cube accurately using observation and sighting techniques.

- The cube is one of the four basic shapes into which objects can be broken down.

- A cube has two cast shadows, the large, obvious one and a thin, dark line under the other side.

in review

1. What are the two effects of linear perspective that are important in drawing?

2. What is the horizon line?

3. When should you use one-point perspective in drawing a cube?

4. When should you use two-point perspective in drawing a cube?

5. What is the difference between one-point and two-point perspective?

6. What is the best way to determine the angles of the horizontal lines when drawing a cube in perspective?

7. What is a good way to check the shape of the top of a cube drawn in perspective?

8. How can you make the edges of a cube appear to come forward toward the viewer?

project

Set up a still life similar to the demonstration . . . using objects that have a cube as their underlying structure: square boxes of various sorts, perhaps your stereo speakers or an unusual container, dice, or boullion cubes. Vary the placement of each, and try to set up at least one object facing you directly so that you can practice drawing in one-point perspective. Using the techniques described in this chapter, draw these objects in charcoal, establishing the correct perspective and rendering accurate values for the light and dark areas. Don't forget the second cast shadow under each cube. Take three hours to complete this drawing.

homework

Using your graphite pencils and 11 × 14 cold-press paper, practice drawing four individual cubic objects of your choice. Be sure to make front edges larger than back edges and to shade the objects realistically to give the illusion of volume.

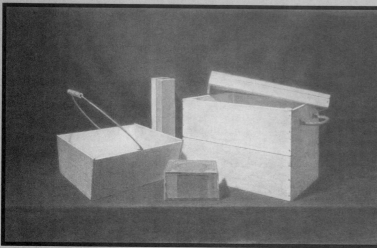

Proportion and Rectangular Shapes

Objectives:

Understand proportion and use it to draw rectangular objects.

Define the horizon plane and be able to draw all the objects in a still life on the same horizon plane.

Use shading and contrast to clearly define the shape and volume of rectangular objects.

Introduction

In the process of learning to draw rectangular objects—a variation of the cube—in this chapter, you'll also learn how knowledge of proportion and understanding of the horizon plane can help you make your drawings more realistic.

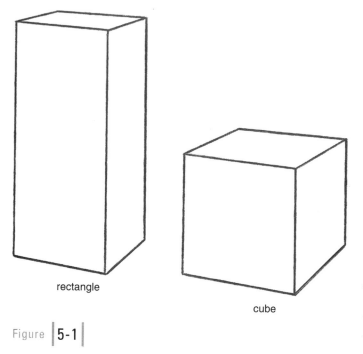

rectangle

cube

Figure **5-1**

PROPORTION

In a perfect cube, all sides are the same size. However, most objects that have the cube as their basic geometric shape are not cubic at all; they are rectangular, like the box on the left in Figure 5-1. In a rectangular object, not all of the planes are the same size. To draw rectangular objects realistically, you must accurately render not only the perspective but also the **proportion** of the object: the differences in size among the height, width, and depth. It's easy to lose the proportions of the object as you struggle to get the perspective correct—and then the object you've drawn doesn't look like what you're seeing. To compound the problem, the proportions of the next object you draw in relation to that first one will be off as well.

Drawing in Proportion

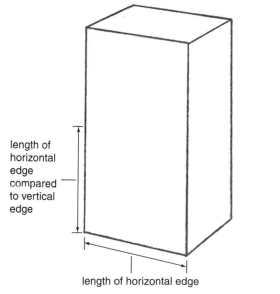

height of the rectangle is two times the width of the left plane

length of horizontal edge compared to vertical edge

length of horizontal edge

Figure **5-2**

To keep your proportions correct, carefully observe the rectangular object you want to draw. Is it taller than it is wide? Is it deeper or wider than it is tall? Use sighting and measuring techniques—not what you know about the object—to answer these questions. Figure 5-2 illustrates the kind of measurements you might make. Start your drawing by establishing a vertical edge, and then carefully align the angles leading away from that edge, as you did with the cube. Measure with your drawing instrument to determine the correct proportions of the object as it appears from your angle of view. Establish the size of one side or plane at a time, and compare each with the last before proceeding to the next.

The Horizon Plane

In a realistic drawing, all of the objects must look as if they all belong to the same environment. They don't all have to have the same basic shape or subject matter, but they do all have to look as if they are all in the same place and being viewed from the same angle. One element that unites a drawing is the horizon line, which is the same as your eye level. As explained in Chap-

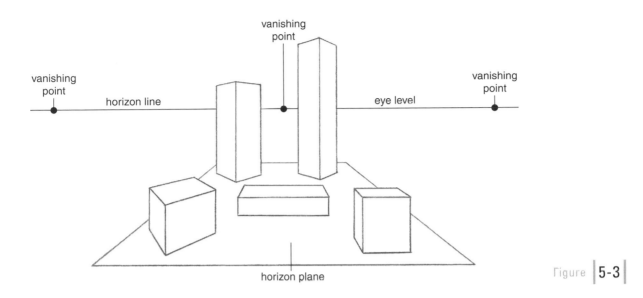

vanishing
point

vanishing
point

horizon line

vanishing
point

eye level

vanishing
point

horizon plane

Figure | 5-3 |

ter 4, the fact that the horizontal lines in all the objects in a drawing converge toward one or two vanishing points not only creates a sense of spatial depth but also unifies the drawing by establishing a single point from which the objects are being viewed.

Figure 5-3 shows a series of rectangular objects on the same **horizon plane.** The horizon plane extends outward from your feet to your eye level in the distance. Both the table and the boxes that sit on it in Figure 5-3 sit on top of the horizon plane, which is created by your eye level. If your still-life drawing focuses only on what's on the table, so that neither the shape of the table nor any other object in the room is visible, you have zeroed in on only a small portion of the entire horizon plane. Both the table and the objects on it must all sit on the same horizon plane, or else your drawing will not look realistic, even if each of the objects looks real by itself.

A practical application of this concept is shown in Figure 5-4, a sketch of the objects in this chapter's illustrated demonstration. You can tell how close or far a rectangular object is from your eye level or horizon line by comparing the sizes of the tops of the objects (if you've viewing them

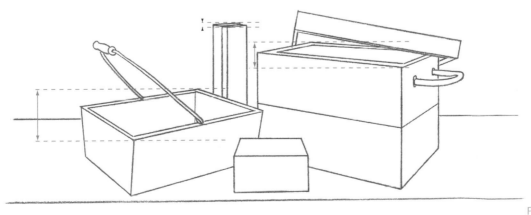

Figure | 5-4 |

from above). The closer the rectangular object is to your eye level, the less of the top you will see. In Figure 5-4, you can see quite a lot of the top of the basket on the left because it is well below your eye level. On the other hand, the top of the tall rectangle is at eye level; you can barely see it. The top of an object viewed from above proportionately increases or decreases according to its relation to your eye level. Nevertheless, no matter what the angle or height of a given object, it must always rest on the same horizon plane as all the other objects.

RECTANGULAR SHAPES

The rectangle is not one of the four basic shapes; rather, it is a variation of a cube. In order to draw rectangular shapes correctly, you must not only understand linear perspective but also determine the proportions that make up the individual rectangle. Thousands of objects, like the cereal box shown in Figure 5-5, are rectangular in shape, so once you know how to draw a rectangle, you'll have control of a lot of different kinds of objects in your drawings. As with a sphere or a cube, you begin by drawing the basic shape, in this case a rectangular one. Then you modify the rectangle as necessary to give its basic shape the individual characteristics of the object you see—for instance, do the sides of the basket with the handle slope slightly rather than being perfectly straight? Next, you give the object volume by shading it, and finally you add details.

Observing the Rectangular Form

A rectangle, like a cube, has six sides. Beyond the fact that all of these sides are *not* the same size, there are an infinite number of variations in the proportions of a rectangle's planes; a rec-

Figure | 5-5 |

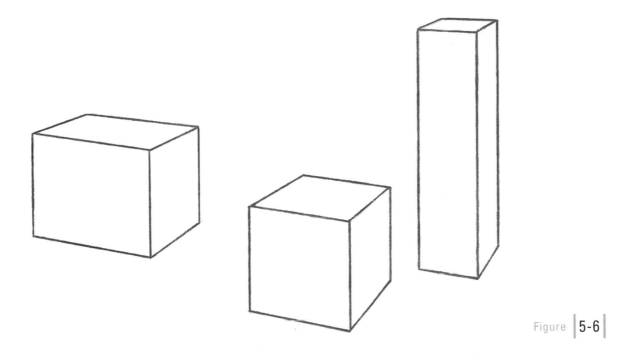

Figure |5-6|

tangular shape may be short, wide, and deep; or tall, wide, and not quite as deep, and so on. Figure 5-6 shows just two variations, in comparison with a cube.

The line drawings in Figure 5-6 have some illusion of depth, but the shaded drawings in Figure 5-7 look much more realistic. A direct source of light reveals the form of an object most clearly, and the drawings in Figure 5-7 capture the effect of a direct light source: You can distinguish light areas from shadow areas, and both from the cast shadow. As in drawing a cube,

Figure |5-7|

you must make the edges that are closest to you come forward while those farther away recede. You can do this partly by making sure that the closer edges are larger, proportionately, than the farther ones and partly by establishing contrast on the sides that form the closer edges. The greater the contrast in values between the two planes, the more that edge will appear to come forward and the more square your rectangle will look.

Drawing Rectangular Objects

You know by now that every drawing begins with observation. Look at the rectangular form in Figure 5-8. This rectangle is set up vertically; that is, it is taller than it is wide. From this angle of view, the front plane is wider than the side plane; the side is only about one-third the size of the front. Since you can see two sides (in addition to the top), you will draw this object in two-point perspective. Your eye level is above the rectangle, because you can see the top, but it's not very far above. The depth of the top plane appears to be only about one twenty-fourth of the size of the height of the front plane.

Figure | 5-8 |

The light is coming from the left and above, so that the top of the rectangle is the light area. As is usual in light areas, there is some gradation in value on the top plane. The highlight, which is always a straight line from the center of the light source, is along the front edge. As with the cube, the contrast between the highlight and the shadow area directly below it not only separates the top and front planes but also pulls the front-top edge forward. The shadow areas are the sides, the two vertical planes. Though both shadow areas are distinct from the light area on the top, there is not much difference in value between the two sides. Yet the edge between them, the one between the two sides you can see, is the edge that is closest to the viewer's eye, so you must make it come forward. If you look carefully, you can see that there is some reflected light in both sides. The left part of the side plane—the part closest to the forward edge—is somewhat darker than its right part, and the right part of the front plane is somewhat lighter than its left part. That's the contrast you can use to make the front edge come forward toward the viewer's eye. As usual, none of the values in the shadow area are as light as those in the light area on top of the rectangle.

As with the cube, the cast shadow wraps under the front plane around to the side and then to the back. The shape of the cast shadow echoes that of the object. The part of the cast shadow that is directly under the front plane appears merely as a thin, dark line. Drawing that dark line helps make the rectangular object sit firmly on its surface. The rest of the cast shadow more obviously takes the form of a rectangle. To establish the cast shadow, use sighting techniques to carefully transfer the angle you see to your drawing. This angle will, of course, vary with the position of the light source. As with any object, the darkest part of the cast shadow is directly under the rectangular form, while the rest of the cast shadow receives a greater or lesser amount of reflected light. There is, however, one important variation in the appearance of the cast shadow between a cube and a rectangular object. Notice that the top edge of the cast shadow is somewhat diffuse and softer than the other edges. This effect is due to the distance between the top of the object and its cast shadow. The taller the rectangular object, the more diffuse that top edge of the cast shadow will be.

SUMMARY

You've just expanded your repertoire of cubic objects to include rectangular shapes, which are, after all, far more common in still-life subjects than are cubes. You used the same perspective techniques you learned for cubes to draw rectangular objects. If you carefully measure the proportions of one rectangular plane to another, and make sure that all of your objects sit on the same horizon plane, you can make any rectangular object look realistic. In the next chapter, you'll learn about a new aspect of the concept of perspective—elliptical perspective—and take on the third of the four basic shapes, the cylinder.

Illustrated Demonstration

Rectangular Objects Still Life

This demonstration of a still-life drawing of rectangular shapes follows the same steps as the demonstration for drawing cubes. You'll see that many of the techniques are similar to those for drawing cubic objects.

Step 1 | **Look.**

I begin by observing my subject and making my mental notes. I see rectangular objects of various sizes on a dark background. The lid of the largest box is at an angle to the box; it is, in effect, another rectangular object to be drawn. Three of the boxes are wider than they are tall—they're placed horizontally—while the backmost box is placed vertically. I can see into the open boxes—in effect, I can see the tops of the objects when I see them as simple rectangular shapes—so I know my eye level is above them. However, I cannot see any of the top of the tall box, it appears almost as a line, so my eye level is there. Most of the boxes are in two-point perspective, except for the one in the center, which is one-point perspective, and the lid, which is in multi-point perspective due to the angle.

The light is coming from the left and slightly above the scene. The two largest objects are quite a bit lighter in value than the background, while the smaller objects are darker than the bigger ones but still lighter than the background. The light areas are the tops (or insides) of the boxes. The shadow areas of the objects are the side planes; the right side planes are darker than the left side planes. There is reflected light in the right part of the right-side planes. The cast shadows start as a thin line directly under the left plane of each object and then wrap around to the right and back.

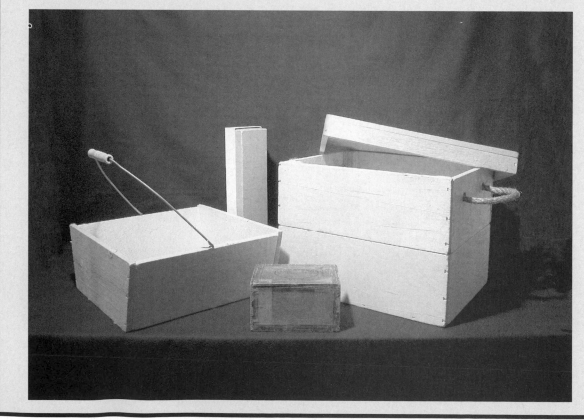

Step 2 | **Transfer the Information.**

I position the still life as a whole on the paper by making my marks of the outer edges. Then I lightly sketch-in loose rectangular shapes for each object for position and size. Once that's done, I draw in each box by transferring the information that I see to the paper by sighting and measuring techniques. Starting with the largest box on the right, which is in two-point perspective, I draw the bottom box first and then draw the lid on top of it. I can use the bottom box as reference for the lid. The lid is in multi-point perspective, so the vertical lines are not perpendicular to the tabletop like the rest of the other vertical lines. I transfer all of the angles of the lid. Then I draw in the handle, which is an irregular shape. This is the object that I will use to draw the other objects in relation to. Like the tissue from the previous demonstration, I transfer all the angles, modify it, and draw it in relation to the side of the box. From there I draw the basket with the handle to the left, in two-point perspective, in relation to the larger box. The sides of the basket taper downward from the top. This is not due to perspective, but is the characteristic of this particular basket. Around the top edge, I draw the inner edge for the thickness of the sides. Then I draw in the handle after the basket is done, beginning with the wire part. I transfer the angles and sight and measure it to the basket. For the wooden handle, I treat it like another rectangle in two-point perspective, but round off the edges. Next, I choose to draw the tall box, again in two-point perspective. This is a much easier task now that the other two boxes are completed on either side of it. I draw it in relation to both boxes and also use the negative space for positioning. Finally, I draw the box that is closest to me. This one is seen in one-point perspective. I draw it in relation to the other boxes. Now I draw in the line for the back edge of the table. I'll put the front edge in later. I step back to look at the drawing and the subject together and make any additional adjustments as necessary.

Step 3 | **Block in the Background.**

Now it's time I turn my vine charcoal on its side and switch my thinking to tone rather than line. Since the background is so dark, I'll eventually have to go darker than I can manage with vine charcoal, but for now I just want to cover up a lot of white paper and begin to eliminate the lines I drew for the edges of the boxes. The tabletop is receiving just a little more direct light than is the background; I squint to see how much lighter the table is and block-in a lighter value for now. I blend both values with my finger or stump and then use a kneaded eraser to reestablish the edges of my objects, if necessary. The result is shown above.

Continues

Illustrated Demonstration

Continued

Step 4 | **Block in the Tones.**

With my vine charcoal, I block in tones for the values of the shadow areas of the two larger boxes, leaving white paper for the highlights. For the two smaller boxes, I first block in tones for the local values, then the shadow areas. I squint to make sure I'm capturing the tones correctly. Then I turn my attention to the cast shadows, determining their angles in relation to their objects. Since the background tones are so dark, I know I'm going to have to darken the cast shadows later, but for now the feeling of light and shadow, as shown here, is what I'm trying to achieve.

Step 5 | **Create Volume.**

It never hurts to reestablish the value scale at this point, by squinting. With this scale in mind, I start to darken the shadow areas on each box. To make the boxes look square, I bring the front edges forward by darkening the shadow areas along those edges to increase the contrast. In the same way, I establish the contrast between the top of each box and the shadow plane by darkening the shadow area near the top; the original tone I blocked-in now becomes the area of reflected light within the shadow area. I also darken the cast shadows directly under the objects.

There's something new in this still life: some of the objects have insides, which also have to be shaded correctly in order to suggest volume. The inside of the box to the left is really the part of light area due to the angle of the light. The volume of the inside of the box is square, too, and is rendered in the same way as the outside, except the values are much lighter. The lid of the box to the right is casting a shadow over the inside of the box. This shadow is much lighter than other cast shadows you have seen. There is space between the lid and the inside of the box and this allows for the value of this shadow to lighten.

The handle on the box (basket) at left also has its own light and shadow areas. I darken the front wire toward the junction to the box, but note that as the handle moves upward, it catches the light. I use a kneaded eraser to remove charcoal from the top of the wire. The reverse happens on the back wire: the dark part is at the top and the light part is at the bottom near the box. On the handle proper, I darken the small shadow areas and then reestablish the light area with the eraser.

I'm almost done with this step. I draw the rope handle on the box at the right. Part of it is in shadow and part of it is in light. Finally, I darken the background and the tabletop around some objects in order to increase the contrast and therefore bring those objects forward. I step back once again to see my drawing, observing which areas I want to darken in the next step.

Step 6   **Finish the Drawing.**

The darkest parts of my drawing are now only about value 6, which is all that vine charcoal can achieve. I'll use the compressed charcoal to establish my values from 7 through 10. Squinting often, I move from compressed charcoal to vine charcoal to kneaded eraser and back as necessary to ensure that the values I've drawn are the values I see. Now I add the front edge of the table, making the dark plane down in front.

Then I fill in details such as the nails in the lidded box and the box with the rope handle, the weave of the rope handle, and the faint ellipse on the top of the box in the front. I darken the top of the table to increase the contrast to really make the boxes stand out. I also make sure it's just a little lighter right along the front edge of the table to pull that forward. One more time I step back and adjust if necessary, then I sign it and apply fixative to the drawing.

things to remember

- A sense of proportion helps you draw objects realistically by establishing the relationships among its height, width, and depth.

- Sighting to compare the apparent size of one plane with that of another will help you establish correct proportions.

- The horizon plane is an imaginary flat surface extending from your feet to your eye level or horizon line.

- Every object in a drawing must sit on the same horizon plane.

- The rectangular object is a variation of the cube.

- Like a cube, a rectangular shape has six sides, but those sides are not all equal.

in review

1. What is the meaning of the term *proportion?*

2. What is the horizon plane?

3. How does the horizon plane help to unify your drawing?

4. How is a rectangular object similar to and different from a cubic object?

5. How is shading used to define the squareness of a rectangular object's edges?

6. How can you make a cubic or rectangular object appear to sit firmly on its surface?

project

Set up a still life composed entirely of rectangular objects, as in the demonstration in this chapter. Choose books, videotapes, a calculator, or boxes of almost any kind—there are so many kinds of rectangular objects that you should have no trouble finding a variety of objects of differing proportions. Arrange them so that they are seen from different angles, and try to set up at least one tall box so that you can't see the top of it. Draw, following the steps of the demonstration, in charcoal on newsprint, taking three hours for the entire process. Remember to pace yourself so that you don't reach the end of your time with only two objects drawn in detail!

homework

Switch to pencil and cold-press paper to make four tonal drawings of individual rectangular objects you choose from among the many such objects you can find in your home. Use white for the background value.

notes

Elliptical Perspective and Cylindrical Objects

Objectives:

Understand elliptical perspective and describe its use in drawing.

Draw an accurate freehand ellipse.

See the underlying cylindrical form of objects in order to simplify their shape.

Draw cylindrical objects, whether they are standing up or lying down, accurately and with a sense of the object's volume.

Introduction

You've mastered two of the four basic shapes and are ready to move on to the cylinder. In order to draw objects that have a cylinder as their underlying shape, you'll need to understand what elliptical perspective is and how it will help you draw realistic-looking cylindrical objects. The cylindrical form poses a lot of potential pitfalls for the beginning artist, but this chapter will tell you how to avoid every one of them.

ELLIPTICAL PERSPECTIVE

The visual phenomenon that allows us to perceive spatial depth in a cube or rectangle also affects objects that have a circle on one or both ends, such as cylindrical and conic shapes. To draw such objects realistically, you must perceive the **elliptical perspective,** the way the shape of the circle changes as your eye level changes.

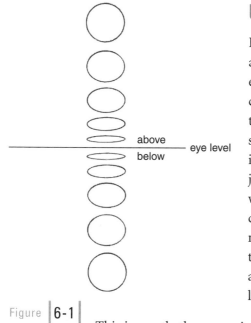

Figure |6-1|

Understanding Elliptical Perspective

Figure 6-1 illustrates elliptical perspective. Seen from directly above or below, the circle remains a circle—or, a perfectly round ellipse, since a circle is one form of ellipse. As your eye level comes closer to the edge of the circle, you see it first as a wide oval and then as a narrower and narrower oval until, finally, if you see it straight on, the front and back edge would merge and all you see is a straight line. Illustrate this for yourself with a cylindrical object such as an empty paper towel roll. Hold the roll as if you wanted to look through it like a telescope. The end appears as a circle. Now rotate the roll in your hand so that you see more and more of the cardboard side. As you do, you'll see that the ellipse on the end becomes narrower and narrower, until finally it becomes a single straight line. The closer your eye level is to the ellipse, the less space you see between the back and the front edge.

This is exactly the same visual phenomenon you observed in studying cubes and rectangles. The ellipse changes shape as your eye level changes, in the same manner as the top of a cube, seen in one-point perspective, changes shape as it comes closer to being at eye level. This similarity is shown in Figure 6-2. The difference, of course, is that the ellipse has no corners; it is a continuous curved line. Therefore, you don't have to worry about vanishing points on the horizon because there are no converging parallel lines.

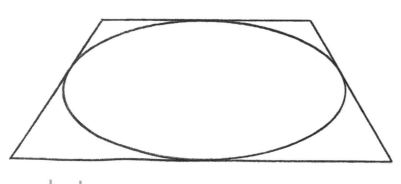

Figure |6-2|

Drawing an Ellipse

In order to draw the cylinder, the basic shape you'll study in this chapter—as well as the cone, which you'll study in the next chapter—you must first learn to draw a reasonably accurate freehand ellipse. You could use a template to make a perfect ellipse, but you don't really need that kind of accuracy in still-life drawing. Anyway, how likely is it that the templates you have available will exactly correspond to the sizes and shapes of the ellipses you'll see in the objects you draw?

Here's a method for drawing accurate ellipses. If your drawing pad is in an upright position, hold your drawing instrument loosely between your thumb and index finger, with the charcoal resting on your index finger and with the tip extending just past the end of your finger. Using your arm, not your wrist, make a sweeping motion to lightly draw the top arc, moving from the narrowest point at one end of the ellipse to the other narrowest point. Correct this arc by going over it lightly several times with short, sweeping strokes. Repeat this procedure for the bottom arc. Finally, connect the top arc and the bottom arc, again using short, sweeping strokes to draw the curve of the narrowest part of the oval where the top and bottom arcs meet. Draw over the shape until it looks like the ellipse you're seeing. The result is a drawing something like Figure 6-3.

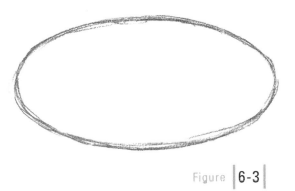

Figure | **6-3** |

If your drawing pad is at an angle or in a horizontal position rather than being upright, then hold your drawing instrument as you would a pencil and, using your wrist rather than your arm, follow the same steps as the previous procedure.

Don't expect to get a perfect ellipse the first or second time. Your first efforts may be lopsided. But, as in drawing a circle, you can make several light lines until the overall shape matches the one you're seeing. Since there are no outlines in reality, only edges, it doesn't matter if you have extra lines; they'll all become part of the background tone in the end.

CYLINDRICAL SHAPES

The third of the four basic shapes is the cylinder. A roll of paper towels is a purely cylindrical shape, and there are many objects, such as the coffee mug shown in Figure 6-4, that are based on the cylinder. Once you can see the cylinder in the underlying shape of an object, you have simplified the object so that you can begin to draw it. You start by drawing a basic cylinder, and then modify it as necessary. Then you give it volume, and add the details last.

Understanding the Cylindrical Form

Cylinders have straight sides that are parallel to each other. Both ends are circles, or perfectly round ellipses. Cylinders can be narrow or wide, short or tall; Figure 6-5 shows just two of the many variations.

The volume of a cylinder is essentially round except for the ends, the ellipse planes. Yet you must not let what you know about cylinders in general dictate how you draw the particular cylinder you see in your still-life subject. Both your eye level in relation to the cylinder and the

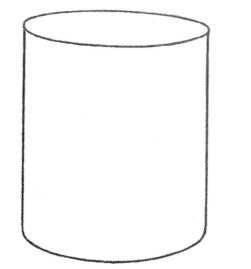

Figure | **6-4** |

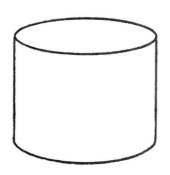

Figure | **6-5** |

angle at which you view it affect the appearance of the cylinder. Accurately drawing a cylinder that is standing upright, like the one on the left in Figure 6-6, involves observing the appearance of the ends using elliptical perspective. When the cylinder is lying on its side, like the one on the right in Figure 6-6, you'll have to use your understanding of both elliptical and linear perspective in order to draw it accurately.

Let's start with cylinders that are standing upright, like the ones in Figure 6-7. Every cylinder has two ellipses for you to render, the one on the top and the one on the bottom. Unless the cylinder is transpar-

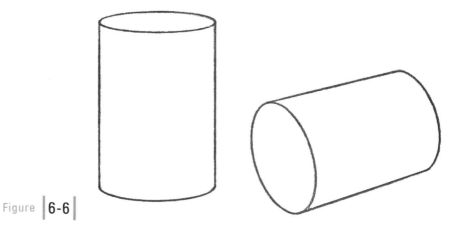

Figure | **6-6** |

ent, you'll see only the front half of one of the ellipses. In Figure 6-7 you see only half of the ellipse
on the bottom; the part you don't see is indicated by
the dotted lines. There is space between the two ellipses of any given cylinder; they are separated by the
sides of the cylinder. Thus, the two ellipses are at different distances from your eye level, and therefore
their shapes will be somewhat different. If the cylinder is short, like the one on the right in Figure 6-7,
then the ellipses are only slightly different from
each other. The difference is far more apparent
when the cylinder is tall, like the one on the left in
Figure 6-7. Notice that the top ellipse, which is
closer to your eye level, is much narrower than the
bottom ellipse, which is farther from your eye level.

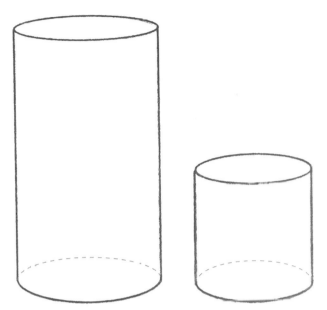

The situation gets more complicated when the cylin-
der is lying on its side and at an angle, as in Figure 6-8. Remember, the sides of a cylinder create
parallel lines. These lines appear to recede into the distance just like the lines in a cube or rectangle. Notice how this affects the size and shape of the ellipses at either end of the cylinder. The
one closest to you is narrower and less round than the one farther away. Not only that, but the
farther ellipse, like any object of the same size that is farther away, appears smaller than the
nearer ellipse. Your mind knows that both those ellipses are the same size and shape. Yet you
must draw not what you know, only what you see.

Figure 6-7

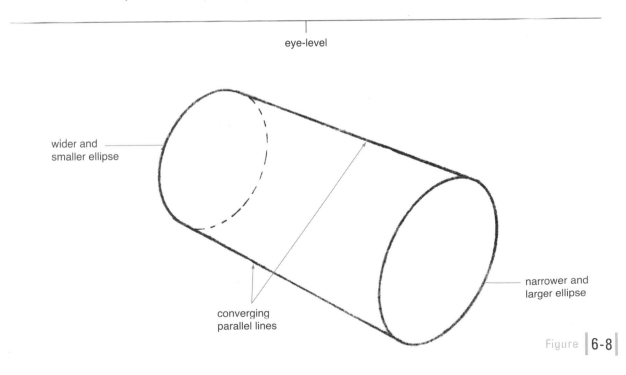

eye-level

wider and smaller ellipse

converging parallel lines

narrower and larger ellipse

Figure 6-8

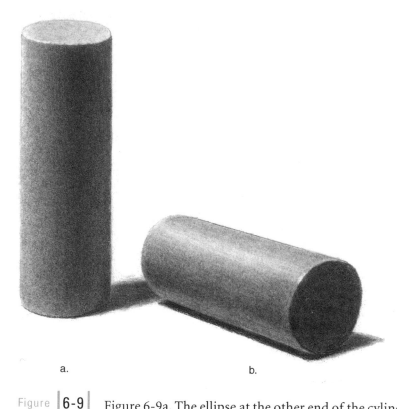

a.   b.

Figure | 6-9 | Figure 6-9a. The ellipse at the other end of the cylinder on its side appears narrower because it is closer to your eye level.

In Figure 6-9, you see two cylinders, one upright and one on its side. Your eye level is somewhat higher than the cylinders. These two cylinders are the same size and shape, yet they look substantially different. Measure the length of the sides with your pencil. The sides of the upright cylinder, shown in Figure 6-9a, are considerably longer than those of the one seen at an angle, Figure 6-9b. That's the effect of linear perspective. Now look at the differences in the shapes of the ellipses. On the upright cylinder, the top ellipse, being closer to your eye level, is slightly narrower than the bottom ellipse. But compare that top ellipse to the closer ellipse of the cylinder on its side. The closer ellipse of the cylinder in Figure 6-9b is wider than the top ellipse of cylinder in

Now look at the way the light creates the form and volume of the two cylinders in Figure 6-9. A strong, direct light hits both cylinders from above and to the left. The portions of the cylinders in the direct path of the light are, naturally, the light areas. In Figure 6-9a, the top ellipse is the light area, and the highlight is along the front edge of the top ellipse (similar to what you see in a cube or rectangular shape). In Figure 6-9b, the light area runs along the top of the length of the cylinder. The highlight is on the edge in the light area as the form meets the flat plane of the ellipse. Note that even in the light area the tones are gradated, though none of the values in this area are as dark as the lightest tones in the shadow area.

The shadow area on the upright cylinder is the entire front of the length of the cylinder. Being closer to the light, the left side is lighter, while the right area is a darker value. The darkest part of the shadow is the area where the side begins to curve around toward the back, which is also the area that is closest to the viewer's eye. In that way the cylinder is like the sphere. Toward the back of the shadow area, reflected light makes the shadow area less dark. The cylinder on its side has two shadow areas: one runs along the length of the cylinder as it curves down toward the tabletop, and the other is the flat plane of the front ellipse. As with all shadow areas, reflected light affects the value of some areas, particularly those closest to the surface on which the cylinder rests.

The cast shadow on both objects behaves like that of a cubic or rectangular object. In addition to the main cast shadow behind the object, there is a dark line under the front of each of the objects. In the case of the upright cylinder, the cast shadow runs from that dark line under the front ellipse around to the back and right. The center of the cast shadow is somewhat lighter than the edges due to reflected light. The cast shadow of the cylinder in Figure 6-9b is similar in many respects, but note that the dark shadow under the side is larger—a thicker line—than the one on the upright cylinder. The curve of the cylinder's side toward the surface leaves this larger cast shadow.

Drawing Cylindrical Objects

As with any of the basic shapes, your observations of the characteristics of the shape inform the process of drawing that shape. One of the most important things to remember in drawing cylinders is that you must carefully observe both of the ellipses that form the ends. Beginning drawing students often make the mistake of drawing exactly the same ellipse for both ends. If you look back at Figure 6-7, you'll remember why this isn't possible—the two ellipses are at different distances from your eye level. The taller the cylinder, the less realistic your drawing will look if you make the two ellipses the same.

Drawing Upright Cylinders

Another common mistake is drawing the ellipse that rests on the surface as a straight line, as in the drawing on the left in Figure 6-10. Though it's true that you can't see the whole ellipse because half of it is behind the object, the half you *can* see is a curved line. The only way you would see the ellipse resting on the surface as a straight line would be if your eye level was exactly at the level of the place where the cylinder meets the surface, as in the drawing on the

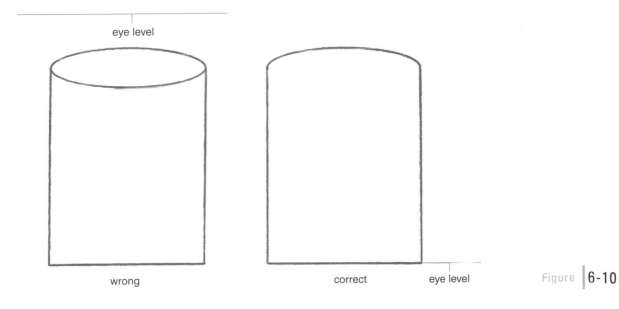

eye level

wrong   correct   eye level

Figure **6-10**

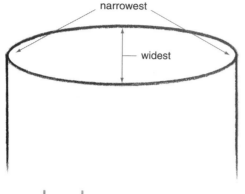

Figure **6-11**

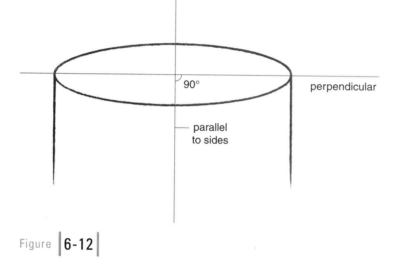

Figure **6-12**

right in Figure 6-10. In this case, you are in effect looking *up* at the rest of the cylinder. You therefore can see only one edge of the ellipse on top. Note the change in eye level between the cylinder on the left, seen from above, and the cylinder on the right, seen from the level of the surface on which the cylinder rests. You can tell that these two objects don't belong together because they're not seen from the same eye level and don't rest on the same horizon plane.

The ellipse is always narrowest at the points where it meets the straight lines that form the sides of the cylinder. It is widest in the middle, between the two sides, as shown in Figure 6-11. To avoid drawing lopsided ellipses, think of imaginary straight lines—or lightly draw in actual lines, which you can erase later—representing the two axes of the ellipse, as in Figure 6-12. One line runs perpendicular to the sides of the cylinder and intersects the cylinder at the two points where the ellipse and the sides meet. The other line, parallel to the sides, is exactly between the intersection point and represents the widest part of the ellipse. These lines will help you draw the ellipse accurately in relation to the sides of the cylinder.

Drawing Cylinders on Their Sides

When the cylinder is placed on its side and you're viewing it from an angle, the ellipses are now at an angle as well. The ellipses remain perpendicular to the sides of the cylinder, but now the lines that delineate the sides are converging toward a vanishing point due to linear perspective. In order to make the ellipses perpendicular to the sides of the cylinder, draw a line down the middle of the cylinder, parallel to the lines for the sides and converging to the same vanishing point, as shown in Figure 6-13. This line is just like the axle on the wheels of a car, connecting two circles through the center point.

Establish this guide line or central axis *before* you begin to draw the cylinder, using sighting techniques. Hold your drawing instrument at an angle so it runs the center length of the cylinder like an axle through the two ellipses. Transfer that angle to the paper, *and then* sight and transfer the angles for each of the sides of the cylinder. Now you have the points where the ellipses will meet the sides. Next, for each of the two ellipses, draw a line perpendicular to the axis line to tell you the angle of the ellipse. The widest part of the ellipse will be along the axis line, and the narrowest parts will meet the sides of the cylinder at the line perpendicular to the axis line. Now you can draw both ellipses using these two lines as guides.

You must also establish the width of the widest part of the ellipse. This procedure is similar to the process of establishing the width of the top of a cubic or rectangular object. You can start by noting your eye level: The far-ther your eye level is above or below the ellipse, the wider the ellipse will appear. But don't stop there; use sighting techniques to measure the length of the widest part of the ellipse as a proportion of the length of the sides of the cylinder. In Figure 6-14, for example, the widest part of the ellipse is approximately one fourth of the length of the cylinder. Two marks on the central axis for the front and back edge of the ellipse will guide you in drawing the el-lipse proportionately.

Always use this procedure, especially when drawing complex cylindrical objects. You might be tempted to skip drawing the guide lines, but the more complex the object, the more im-portant it is that you simplify in this way. If either of the el-lipses looks as if it's drawn from the wrong perspective, your object will be "off"; viewers will see that it doesn't look real-istic, but may not be able to put their finger on why it looks wrong. If you find that something doesn't look right, don't just try to draw over the same lines. Go back to square one, as if you were drawing this object for the first time. Restart by establishing the angle of the central axis, and then go through each of the steps outlined previously in turn.

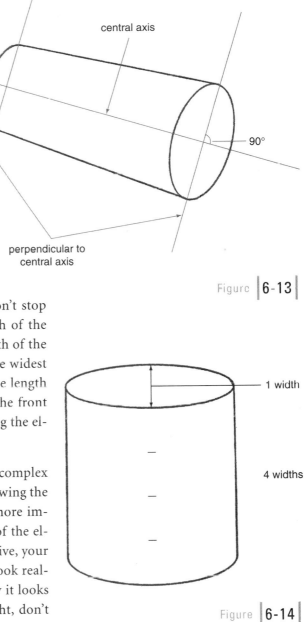

Figure | **6-13** |

Figure | **6-14** |

Establishing Volume

Of course, an accurate line drawing is only the beginning. Now you must give your cylinder volume by filling in the values you observe. Where is the light coming from, and how strong is it? Where are the light areas, the highlights, and the shadow areas? Which are the darkest parts of the shadow areas? Establish your value scale, with value 1 being the highlight (usually the white of the paper) and value 10 being the cast shadow directly under the object. The darkest part of the light area is lighter than the lightest part of the shadow area, and the darkest part of the shadow area is usually lighter than the lightest part of the cast shadow, depending on the local colors of the object and its background.

Establishing values in a cylindrical object combines the techniques used for the sphere and for the cube. Since the side of the cylinder is round, rendering its volume is a lot like drawing a sphere. The greatest contrast in value occurs at the point closest to the viewer's eye, so that this area comes forward. Looking back at Figure 6-9, you'll see that the darkest part of the shadow area comes in the middle of the sides of each of the cylinders, the part closest to your eye. Conversely, the relationship between the ellipse and the side of a cylinder is more like that of the sides of a cubic object. Contrast in value establishes the edge between the top and the sides. In both cylinders shown in Figure 6-9, the greatest contrast occurs at the part of the edge that is closest to the viewer's eye.

SUMMARY

Elliptical perspective is an important part of drawing cylindrical objects so that they look realistic. Even more important than understanding, intellectually, that an ellipse gets narrower as it gets closer to your eye level is the process of observing and measuring the actual ellipses you see before you. Particularly when you're drawing cylindrical objects that are lying on their side and at an angle, establishing guide lines along the central axis and perpendicular to that axis is crucial to your success. Fortunately, you already mastered the techniques for creating the illusion of volume for cylindrical objects when you studied the sphere and the cube. Next, you'll learn to create the illusion of space in a drawing and find out how to render the last of the basic shapes, the cone.

Illustrated Demonstration

Cylindrical Objects Still Life

For this demonstration, we'll concentrate on objects whose basic shape is the cylinder. Adding the cylinder to the repertoire of basic shapes you can draw accurately gives you control over a wide variety of everyday objects; your kitchen, in particular, is full of cylindrical shapes. Each of the cylindrical objects in this demonstration is seen from a different angle, so that you'll get practice in observing and using sighting techniques to render cylinders accurately, no matter how they're placed in relation to your eye. Keep in mind that the farther away an ellipse is from your eye level, the more round it appears to be, especially in taller objects. Be sure to follow all the steps in this demonstration along with me; don't get ahead of yourself by skipping to the next step before the present one is complete.

Step 1 | **Look.**

It's impossible to over-stress the importance of making your observations before you begin to draw. In looking at the still-life set-up, as shown here, I see a variety of cylindrical objects in a grouping whose basic shape is horizontal. A dark cloth is placed both behind and under the objects. The angle of the cast shadows tells me that the light comes from above and to the right. The lightest local value is that of the vase; the next-to-darkest is that of the mug with the lid; the background cloth is the darkest. The lightest values are the highlights, particularly those of the lighter-colored objects; the darkest values, as usual, are in the cast shadows directly under the

Continues

Illustrated Demonstration

Continued

objects and in the darkest part of some of the shadows on the objects. Because I can see the top ellipse of each upright cylinder, I know that my eye level is above the group of objects. The rolling pin is lying on its side at an angle to me; its parallel lines converge upward to my eye level. Finally, I note that some of these objects have reflective surfaces. I'll have to work not only to make the objects round but also to render this reflective quality, paying attention to the size, shape, and value of the reflections themselves. Anything I see reflected in a curved surface is going to have a different shape from the original object.

Step 2 | **Transfer the Information.**

On a horizontal pad, after marking the boundaries of the still-life for position, I rough in cylindrical shapes for the position and size of each object.

Capturing each object in more detail, I start with the milk pail to the left. Being the tallest object, I use it as reference for drawing all of the other objects. I break the pail into three parts and use a vertical centerline to help line up all the parts. First I draw the bottom part, to establish the base. By sighting and measuring, I transfer the angles of the middle shape and position it on top of the base. Now I can draw the top cylinder, making sure the proportions of each shape are accurate. I draw the handle in the same manner as in the other demonstrations. Once that's completed, I measure the negative space between the white vase and the pail to position the vase next to it. Starting with the bottom part, I draw that, then the flared collar, using a horizontal guide line to keep the ellipse from becoming lopsided, and then finally the ridges. To draw the mug to the right, I again start with establishing a center line. I make the long cylinder shape first by referencing it to both previously drawn objects by sighting and measuring. Then I can add the flared bottom and top lip. Notice the difference in the ellipse shapes. Drawing the lid is easy, using the center line and the milk pail as reference to help me. In drawing the handle, I use the negative and positive space for information and measure the top and bottom part of the attachment for positioning. Now that this object is done, I can draw the cup to the extreme right. This is just a simple cylinder, and by sighting and measuring, I draw that in without the ridges. Finally I turn to the rolling pin. First, I need to draw in the center line by sighting. After that, I transfer the angles of the sides of the barrel. By sighting, I mark where the ellipses are for the ends of the barrel and handles using lines perpendicular to the center line. I draw in each ellipse carefully by measuring each shape and using both guide lines. Then I transfer the angles of the shape of the handle. I draw in the line for the back edge of the table and step back to check my work. This is my sketch.

Step 3 | **Block in the Background.**

Squinting to determine values, I block in two main areas of tone with my vine charcoal, darker for the wall and lighter for the tabletop. These tones cover the lines I made for the edges of the objects, so that I now have white objects against a dark background, as shown.

Step 4 | **Block in the Tones.**

The direct light makes it easy to see the differences in value between light and shadow areas. I lightly block in tones to represent the local values of the objects. I leave the vase and the rolling pin white. Then I fill in shadow areas for each of the objects, including the vase and the rolling pin; I squint frequently to compare values in one area to those in another. Then I fill in a tone for the cast shadows, carefully aligning each cast shadow with its object. As I noticed before, the mug has a highly reflective surface. The reflection is of the white vase, but the shape is distorted, due to the curvature of the cylinder. To draw the shape of the reflection, I draw the negative space around the vase by using a darker tone on top of the tone for the local value to make the shape I see. Remember, a reflected light is never as light as a highlight or a tone from the light area. I darken some areas in the background as necessary to make sure I don't lose the edges of my objects. Once again I step back to see that my drawing looks like my subject.

Continues

Illustrated Demonstration

Step 5 | **Create Volume.**

This is where I create the contrast in values that suggests the volume of the objects. I darken the shadow areas of each cylindrical object where they meet the light areas in order to bring that curve forward and give the illusion of roundness. As I do so, I'm suggesting the reflected light in the outside edges without having to lighten any of the tone I've already laid down. Since some of the values in the background and shadow areas are very dark, I now have to add some compressed charcoal, sparingly, to the shadow areas and the background to continue to create the volume.

Besides the reflection on the mug, the vase has a few small reflections as well. To draw these reflections, I repeat how I drew the reflection on the mug. I darken the area around the shape of the reflection and then the lighter tone becomes the shape of the reflection. Also, in the reflection of the vase on the mug, there is a cast shadow on the vase from the mug on the side I can't see. I draw this shape of the shadow as I see it. I continue to squint and compare my values, especially around the reflections. Getting these values accurate will create the volume of the mug with the reflection on it. As I darken the values of the objects, I have to darken the cast shadows and the background as well. There are a few folds in the cloth against the wall catching the light. The shadow areas of the folds are soft and the edges diffused. To create this effect, I use the compressed charcoal to make the shapes of the shadows and blend it in with my fingers. I stop and step back to compare my drawing to the still life, (which now looks like this) to the subject.

Step 6 | **Finish the Drawing.**

Finally, from comparing my drawing to the subject in the last step, I now know where I need to darken or lighten certain areas to finish my drawing. I start by darkening the cloth behind the objects and the tabletop. Then I find that I have to darken the cast shadows. Now all the objects become sharper due to the increase in the values, and they come forward from the background. I add some of the ridges to the small cup on the right and some wood grain to the rolling pin. The trick to adding texture like this is to draw it lightly so the texture becomes part of the volume of the object, rather than distracting or flattening it. Then I switch to the other end of the scale and use my kneaded eraser. The drawing is now completed as shown, and has been signed and sprayed with fixative.

things to remember

- Elliptical perspective is the optical illusion by which an ellipse, such as a circle, seems to narrow as it comes closer to eye level and to widen as it gets farther away.

- A cylinder, one of the four basic shapes, combines the attributes of the sphere and the cube.

- The ends, or ellipses, of a cylinder are perpendicular to the sides.

- The two ellipses of a cylinder will never appear identical in shape because one is closer to your eye level than the other.

- When a cylinder is lying on its side and at an angle to you, linear perspective makes the sides appear to converge toward your eye level.

- Draw guide lines, a central axis, and a line perpendicular to that axis to help you accurately render the ellipses of a cylinder that is lying on its side.

- The illusion of volume in a cylinder comes from the contrast in value between the ellipses and the sides and between the light and shadow areas of the sides.

in review

1. What is elliptical perspective?

2. What is the appearance of a circle, such as the end of a cylinder, when it is seen from exactly eye level?

3. How is drawing a cylinder similar to drawing a sphere?

4. How is drawing a cylinder similar to drawing a cube?

5. What effect does linear perspective have on a cylinder lying on its side and at an angle?

6. What is the first step in drawing a cylinder lying on its side and at an angle?

7. What happens to the ellipses of a cylinder that is lying on its side and at an angle?

project

As in the previous chapters, set up a still life, this time composed entirely of cylindrical objects. Choose objects of various colors so that you can practice rendering volume in a variety of local colors. Make sure you place at least one object on its side and at an angle to you so that you can practice the many steps necessary to render such objects realistically. Try using a different background or angle of light than you used in the previous project. Take three hours to complete a still-life drawing in charcoal on newsprint.

homework

Find four cylindrical objects you would like to draw in pencil. When you draw them, see the cylinder in each object, and follow the steps outlined in this chapter to accurately render them. Again, use white as the value for the background.

The Illusion of Space and Conical Shapes

Objectives:

Create the illusion of space in drawing by using relative size, vertical placement on the page, overlapping of objects, and contrast in values.

Establish a foreground, middle ground, and background in drawings.

Perceive the underlying conical shape of many everyday objects.

Create an accurate line drawing of a cone, whether it is standing upright or lying on its side.

Render the volume of a conical object using shading.

Introduction

You've learned in previous chapters to create the illusion of volume in the objects you draw by using linear and elliptical perspective and by shading objects to show how the light reveals their form. Now it's time to learn to create the illusion of *space,* the distance between objects. In this chapter, you'll learn several surefire techniques for showing the relative distance of objects from the viewer's eye. You'll also learn to draw the cone, the last of the four basic shapes.

THE ILLUSION OF SPACE AND CONICAL SHAPES

CREATING THE ILLUSION OF SPACE

Creating the illusion of volume in each individual object is only part of what you need to do in order to make your drawings look realistic. Another important aspect of realistic drawing is accurately depicting the space *between* objects, particularly their relative distance from the viewer's eye. If you look around you at the objects you can see in your immediate surroundings, you can notice the distance between one object and another. Not only do you see the negative space between objects as a shape, but your eye also perceives how far away each object is in relation to another. If you look out a window, this phenomenon is even more obvious—your eye easily perceives the distance between something that is right outside your window and something that is several blocks away. You want to capture this three-dimensional distance in your two-dimensional drawing. Artists have several ways of creating this illusion of space.

Foreground, Middle Ground, and Background

Every drawing—indeed, every scene you can see in real life—has a **foreground,** a **middle ground,** and a **background.** These relative spaces exist in relation to your eye level. The foreground is the area that is close to you, like the space where the tree appears in Figure 7-1. The background is the area that is farthest away, where the mountains are in Figure 7-1. The middle ground is in between, like the fence and row of trees between the large tree and the mountains pictured in Figure 7-1. The differences between foreground, middle ground, and background become more pronounced the larger the scope of what you're drawing; thus, the distance between what is near and what is far away is very noticeable in landscape drawing (see Chapter 13). In a still life, the foreground, middle ground, and background are likely to be very close together, but they are still important for helping you achieve the illusion of space.

Figure | **7-1** |

Size and Placement

You learned in Chapter 4 that size is one way of showing how far an object is from the viewer's eye. The forward edge of a cube looks larger than the back edge, and an apple in your hand looks larger than an apple across the street.

Indicating distance with size works particularly well when two objects are about the same size, like the two edges of a cube or the two apples. Another tool you can use to create the illusion of space when two objects are dramatically different in size is vertical placement on the page. The higher the vertical placement, the farther away the object appears to

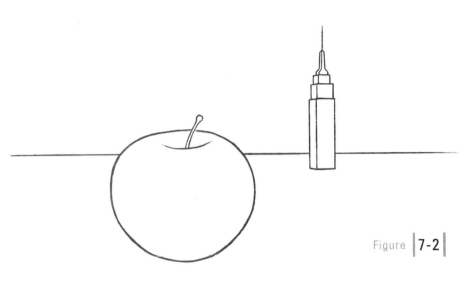

Figure | **7-2** |

be. You know that the skyscraper in Figure 7-2 is much larger than the apple. Yet because the skyscraper is drawn smaller than the apple and because it is placed much closer to the top of the page, you perceive the skyscraper to be farther away than the apple.

This phenomenon works because of your eye level or horizon line. Recall from Chapter 5 how to establish your horizon plane: Look straight ahead and, without moving your head, move your eyes down toward your feet and back up again. Now imagine putting a box around everything that you can see without moving your head. That's your picture frame. Your eye level falls about two-thirds of the way up from your feet within this frame—and that's where the horizon line is drawn in Figure 7-2, two-thirds of the way up the page. Things that are closer to your feet—lower in the picture frame—are perceived to be in the foreground. Things that are closer to the horizon line—higher in the picture frame—are perceived to be in the background, farther away than things that are placed lower on the page. The foreground in most drawings is usually closer to the bottom of the page than the background.

Overlapping Objects

Another way to create the illusion of space is by overlapping objects. When viewing Figure 7-3, you have no trouble perceiving that the

Figure | **7-3** |

Figure | **7-4** |

apple on the left is in front of the apple on the right. The apple that is partially obscured has to be farther away than the one that blocks your view of it. Furthermore, you can tell by the size and vertical placement of the two apples that they are not very far apart. Figure 7-4 shows how to send the second apple into the background: Not only does the closer apple overlap it, but the apple that is farther away is also smaller and placed higher on the page, closer to the horizon line. Combining these effects enables you to clearly establish the illusion of space for the viewer.

Value Contrast

So far we've looked at ways to create the illusion of space that work even in a simple line drawing. Yet you know that creating the illusion of volume depends on rendering a range of values—that principle also applies to creating the illusion of space between objects. You've already learned to increase the range of values in an object in order to bring that area of contrast closer to the viewer's eye. A similar technique works to bring objects in the foreground closer to the viewer's eye than those in the background. The objects that are closest to you in a still life have a greater range of values than those in the background, while those in the middle ground will have a medium range of values. In Figure 7-5, the closer apple appears closer not only because it overlaps the other and is larger and placed lower in the picture frame, but also because it shows a greater range of values than the other apple. The range for the forward apple

Figure | **7-5** |

is values 1–10, while the back apple's range is only about values 1–6. The more extreme the range of values, the more the object appears to come forward in the drawing. The less extreme the range of values—including the contrast with the background—the more the object will recede.

If you could look out the window at the vista shown in Figure 7-1, you'd see the background mountains as a lighter value, with a reduced range, as compared to the tree in the foreground. The tree might have a range of values 1–8 or even larger depending on how close it is to you, while the mountains might have a range of only 2–4. But if you drove by car up to those mountains so that they became your foreground, you would then see a larger range of values in the mountains, while the tree in the distance would have a smaller range.

Why Value Range Affects the Perception of Distance

The reason that objects drawn with a greater range of values appear closer than those with a lesser range has to do with **atmospheric perspective,** a phenomenon related to the amount of light you see bouncing off an object in relation to its distance from you. The farther away an object is, the less of the light you see because of the amount of air between you and the object. Air has density, even though you can see through it. The more air between you and the object, the more distance and density the light rays have to travel through. Since different colors of light rays have different lengths, some of the shorter rays may never reach your eyes. Thus, atmospheric perspective decreases the range of values you see the farther away you are from an object.

Also, a larger range of values is simply easier to see, and your eye is attracted to what it can see most easily. It's easier to see in a well-lit room than in one that is in semidarkness. Indeed, this is why books are usually printed in black ink on white paper—it's easier on the eye. If the words in this book were printed in a medium gray ink, you'd have a harder time reading it because the value of the ink is closer to white, than black. The contrast between the values is less. Your eye and your brain would have to work harder to interpret what you're reading; your eyes would get tired, and you might stop reading. So when an object has a wide range of values, your eye is drawn to it because it's easier to see, and that makes it seem to come forward in the picture plane.

In a still-life drawing, the distance between objects is less extreme than that between the tree and the mountain, but still, the objects in the foreground have a greater range of values than those in the middle ground and yet greater than those in the background. This doesn't mean you can't have a dark object in the background or a light object in the foreground. It just means that a light object in the foreground has to have a greater *range* of values than a dark object in the background. The white cone in Figure 7-6 has a lighter local color than the red apple, but, because it's in the foreground and well lit, it shows a range of values 1–10. The apple, despite its darker color, has a much smaller range of values than does the cone. Using value to create the illusion of space involves contrasting one range of values against another range of values to make the object with the greater range appear to come forward.

When drawing a relatively distant object against a background value, you have to consider the values of the background in relation to those of the object. To make the object recede, keep its range of values as close as you can to the values of the background. For instance, if the background is dark, keep the object's range of values as much on the dark side as possible, even if the local value of the object is light. You don't want to darken the entire object, but emphasize the values in its dark areas to keep them as similar as possible to the background values.

Figure | 7-6 |

The key to creating the illusion of space is to combine all of the techniques just described. By using size, vertical placement, overlapping, and value ranges to establish space among the objects you're drawing, you will get as close as humanly possible to rendering the illusion of three dimensions on your two-dimensional paper.

CONICAL SHAPES

The last of the four basic shapes is the cone. Conical shapes underlie the basic structure of a wide variety of objects, such as the funnel shown in Figure 7-7. When you can see the underlying conical shape of an object, the simplification process in your brain makes it easy to draw a basic cone and then modify it to make it look like the object you're seeing. As usual, you start with an accurate line drawing and then add tone to give the object value, saving the details for last.

Observing the Conical Form

Like the cylinder, the cone combines aspects of the sphere and the cube. The basic volume is round, like that of the sphere. A perfect cone has an ellipse at one end and a point at the other. Where the ellipse plane meets the sides of the cone, you use the same shading techniques as with a cube to bring the nearer edge forward.

Also, like the cylinder, the cone has a different appearance when it is lying on its side from when it is standing upright, as shown in Figure 7-8. Rendering a cone that is lying down requires use of techniques similar to those used with the cylinder.

Putting a source of light on the cone reveals its volume. The light on the cones in Figure 7-8 is coming from the left and above, so the light area of the cone in Figure 7-8a is on its left, and the

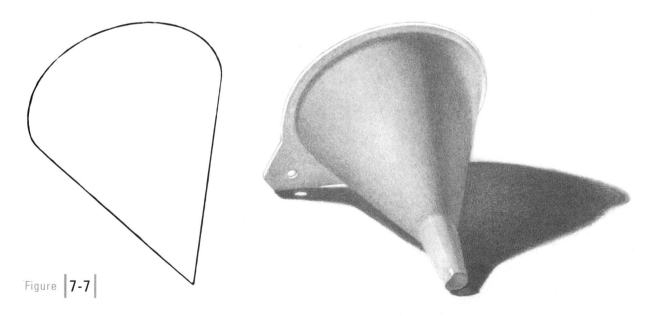

Figure | 7-7 |

light area of the cone in Figure 7-8b is on the flat plane of the ellipse. The area of greatest contrast in both cones is where the light area meets the shadow area; this contrast brings this area forward. On the upright cone, the center is closest to the viewer's eye. On the cone in Figure 7-8b, the base of the cone is even closer to the viewer's eye than is the side, so the greatest contrast in values there is between the elliptical base and the sides. As usual, though there is a range of values in both the light and shadow areas; none of the values in the light areas are as dark as those in the shadow areas. The high-light appears on the part that is in a straight line from the center of the light source.

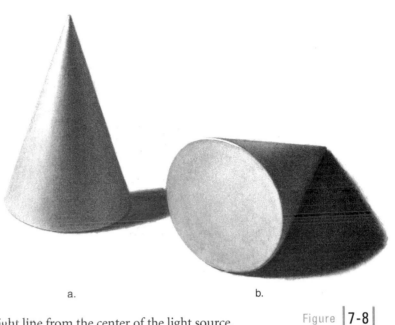

a.   b.

Figure | **7-8** |

The range of values in the cast shadows is as dark or darker than that of the shadow area, with the darkest value, as always, being directly under the object. The shape of the cast shadow mimics that of the object but is not identical; you'll use sighting techniques to accurately render the angle and shape of the cast shadow. The cast shadow of both cones gets more diffuse as it moves farther away from the object.

Drawing Conical Objects

To draw conical objects, you must use not only your observations but also your understanding of elliptical perspective. When the cone is lying on its side, linear perspective will also help you draw it accurately.

Drawing Upright Cones

The biggest pitfall in drawing an upright cone is having it come out lopsided. The best way to prevent a lopsided appearance is to begin by drawing a vertical center guide line from the tip to the middle of the base, as shown in Figure 7-9. This line will ensure that the tip is centered over the base. Determine the proportion of the height of the cone to its width at the base using sighting techniques, and make light marks for the tip and the edges of the base. Then you can

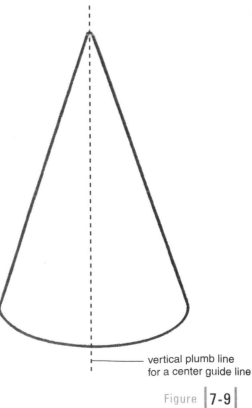

vertical plumb line
for a center guide line

Figure | **7-9** |

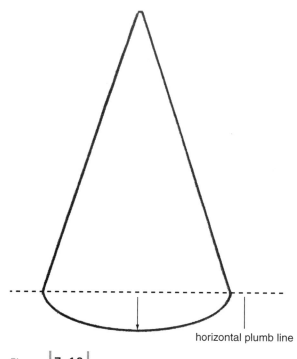

horizontal plumb line

Figure |7-10|

sight the angles of the sides and draw those in. Then, to draw the partial ellipse that forms the base, start by determining where your eye level is in relation to the base. If your eye level is near the base of the cone, the ellipse will be shallower; if your eye level is far above the base of the cone, the ellipse will appear more rounded. Next, use your drawing instrument as a horizontal plumb line from one corner of the base to the other, as shown in Figure 7-10, and determine how far below that line the widest part of the ellipse extends. Now you should be able to draw the ellipse using the technique described in Chapter 6, starting with light strokes and redrawing as necessary until you get the shape right.

After you have an accurate line drawing, you render the volume with tone using the same techniques you employed for the cylinder.

Drawing Cones on Their Sides

Drawing cones that are lying down on their sides, like the ones shown in Figure 7-11, is similar to drawing cylinders on their sides; you have to use linear as well as elliptical perspective. To draw any of the cylinders in Figure 7-11, start with a center guide line, just as you did for the cylinder and the upright cone. This line will help you position the ellipse and the tip in relation to the sides of the cone. Measure the proportions of the length of the sides in relation to the width of the cone and make two light marks on the central guide line to indicate the tip and base of the sides. Next, lightly draw a line perpendicular to the central line for the axis of the ellipse. Determine the proportion of the widest part of the ellipse in relation to the length of the cone. For instance, the width of the ellipse of the cylinder in Figure 7-11a is almost equal to the length of the cone. Mark the widest part of the ellipse on the central guide line. Then determine the depth of the cone by comparing it to the length, and mark this measurement lightly on the perpendicular guide line, keeping the center axis in the middle. Now you can draw the ellipse in light sketching lines, using the marks you made, until it looks correct. After that, transfer the angles of the sides, making sure the length remains correct in proportion to the width.

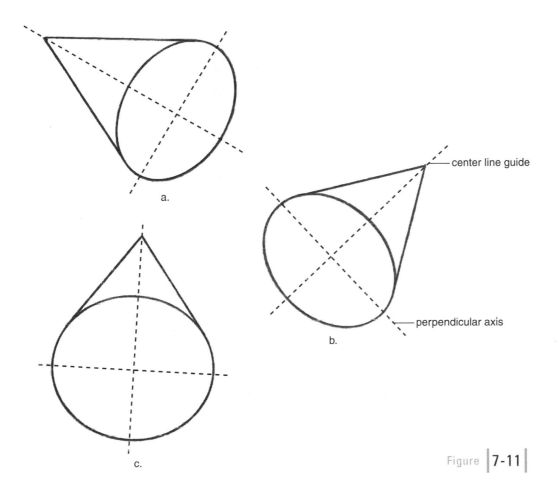

a.

center line guide

perpendicular axis

b.

c.

Figure **7-11**

SUMMARY

Even when you're drawing a subject whose objects are relatively close together, as in a still life, the subtle rendition of the distances between objects is crucial to the illusion of space that makes your drawing look realistic. You learned in this chapter to use size and placement, the overlapping of objects, and the range of values to suggest that objects are nearer or farther away. You also learned to draw the last of the basic shapes, the cone. In the next chapter, you'll put together your knowledge of all four shapes to learn how to draw complex objects that combine more than one shape, as well as learning some of the basic principles of composition that allow you to arrange the objects in your still life in eye-pleasing ways.

Illustrated Demonstration

Conical Objects Still Life

The following is the last demonstration of drawing basic shapes. Once you've added the cone to your repertoire, you will have mastered all of the basic shapes—which means that you have the understanding to be able to draw any object you see!

Step 1 | **Look.**

This still life shows a variety of cone-shaped objects on a medium-value background. Three of the cones are upright (though one of the funnels is upside down, standing on its tip) and two are lying on their sides. The funnel on the left appears almost as a circle; the base is facing me and I can see very little of the sides. My eye level is above the still life, though it's only slightly above the top of the bucket with the handles—I know this because the ellipse of the open top appears very narrow.

The light is from the left and above. The lightest local values are those of the bucket with the handles, the funnel and the cone directly in front of it. The darkest local values are the handle on the side of the bucket and the funnel to the right of it. The darkest values are in the cast shadows directly under the objects and the shadow areas in the handles, and the lightest values are in the highlights on all the objects. The funnel to the right of the bucket is translucent, so that some of the light shines through it. That funnel has its lighter values on its right side and the darker values on the left.

| Step 2 | **Transfer the Information.**

I mark the still life as a whole on my paper and then lightly sketch a cone for each object in relation to the other objects and to the shape of the whole. Then I work on drawing each object accurately.

I start with the bucket because it's largest and in the center. The rest of the objects can be drawn in reference to the bucket. I lightly draw a center guide line to keep my bucket from being lopsided. Though the underlying structure of the bucket is a cone, the point of the cone is cut off so that I see an ellipse at the top. I draw a line perpendicular to the center guide line to help me position the ellipse at the top. Then I transfer the angles of the sides by sighting. I draw the handle on the side by measuring where it attaches to the side. I see the negative space inside the handle to help me draw that shape. Then I can draw the thickness of the handle. To draw the top handle, I measure where the handle attaches along the sides of the ellipse. I transfer the angles of the wire parts of the handle. I measure the distance of the handle from the bucket and make a mark. For the wooden part of the handle, which is a cylinder, I start by drawing a center guide line down the middle. I also draw perpendicular lines to the center guide line to help draw the ellipses at either end. Then I draw the spout of the bucket by sighting and measuring it in reference to the rest of the bucket. Then I lightly draw in the ellipse for the bottom of the bucket.

Starting with the funnel on the right, I measure its position in relation to the bucket, marking the top and the bottom. I lightly draw in a center guide line and one perpendicular to it for the top ellipse. I lightly sketch in the shape of the ellipse, the inside edge first and then the outside edge. The handle on the funnel is a flat cone shape; I use the center guide line to help me draw it in position. Once the ellipse is drawn, I transfer the angles of sides. Then I draw another cone shape for the spout at the bottom, still using the center guide line to position it and the other ellipse at the end. I make sure it is more rounded than the one above since it is further away from my eye level.

The funnel next to the one I've just drawn is lying on its side. I lightly mark its position in relation to the bottom of the bucket and the funnel to the right. I draw a center guide line and perpendicular lines for the ellipses and sketch in the entire shape as I did for the upright funnel, the only difference being that I draw the entire ellipse at the base of the spout. Next, I draw the upright cone, beginning with a light center line, which I sight and measure in relation to the other objects, drawing center and perpendicular lines to transfer the ellipse and then transfering the angles of the sides.

The last funnel is lying at an unusual angle, so I need to take a different approach. I draw a light guide line for the narrowest part of the ellipse, even though it is nearly round. I draw the inner edge of the ellipse and then the outer edge. Seeing the ellipse as a clock face, since it's so nearly round, I position the handle and the spout as hours on the clock. Then I transfer the angles of the sides of the handle and of the spout, also using the bucket to help position the spout. Once all of the objects are done, I draw a straight line for the back edge of the table. I step back and compare my drawing, as shown, to the still life.

Continues

Illustrated Demonstration

Continued

Step 3 | **Block in the Background.**

Laying my vine charcoal on its side, I block in a medium value for the cloth against the wall and a somewhat lighter value for the cloth on the table, squinting to compare these values with the overall value scale I established in Step 1. After I blend the charcoal with my finger or paper stump, I also obscure some of the lines I drew for the edges of the objects, so that I have white objects on a dark background, as shown.

Step 4 | **Block in the Tones.**

Now I start blocking in tones, beginning with the darkest local values. I keep the white of the paper for the highlights for the dark objects and of the light areas of the light-colored objects such as the bucket, the funnel directly in front of it, and the cone. For those objects, I block in only the shadow areas, and then I darken the shadow areas of the darker objects. Finally, I draw in shapes for the cast shadows, sighting the angle at which they sit from their objects. Squinting frequently, I move all over the drawing, darkening areas in relation to what I see. Now my drawing is beginning to have a sense of light and shadow on each object. I step back to compare those values with what I see in my subject.

Step 5 **Create Volume.**

Still using only vine charcoal, I create volume by darkening certain areas to increase contrast with the lighter areas. The contrast between the light and shadow areas of these conical objects needs to be greatest along the curve closest to the viewer, so I darken the shadow areas closest to the light areas. However, due to the translucent nature of the material of the funnels, this alters the range of values in the shadow areas to something different than all the rest of the examples in this book. I have to squint to compare the values in order to still create the form yet capture the translucency of their material. I darken the cast shadows, especially directly under the objects, and I also darken the background directly around the objects, which will make them appear to come forward by contrast. I pay particular attention to places where one object meets or overlaps another, lightening one or darkening the other to make sure I don't lose the edges. When I've increased the range of values as much as I can and am beginning to have a sense of volume for all the objects, it's time to move on to the next step. I step back to see which values need to go darker.

Step 6 **Finish the Drawing.**

I already know where I want to use my compressed charcoal to increase the value scale on the dark side. I darken the cast shadows again, particularly directly under the objects so that they appear to sit firmly on their surface. The range of values should be greatest in the object closest to me, which is the cone in front of the bucket. Notice that with the increased range of values the cone comes forward from the rest of the objects in the picture plane. Also see how the right edge of the shadow side of the bucket recedes backward due to the decreased range of values with the background. I darken the background and along the table line. If necessary, I reestablish highlights using a kneaded eraser. I also darken the tabletop, especially along the bottom edge of the drawing. This helps increase the range of values in contrast to the light areas and pulls those objects forward in the picture plane. I step back to make sure my drawing matches what I am seeing.

things to remember

- Realistic drawing depends not only on the illusion of volume in any given object but also on the illusion of space between objects.

- Objects that are drawn larger appear closer to the viewer's eye than objects that are drawn smaller.

- Placing an object higher in the picture plane makes it appear farther away.

- An object that overlaps another object appears closer than the one it is overlapping.

- Nearby objects have a greater range of values than objects that are farther away.

- Combine size, vertical placement, overlapping, and value range to achieve the illusion of space.

- The cone is one of the four basic shapes.

- Begin with a central guide line in order to draw a cone accurately.

- When a cone is lying on its side, begin with a central guide line and then add a line perpendicular to the central line to represent the widest part of the ellipse.

- Since the volume of the cone is essentially round, shade it as you would a cylinder.

in review

1. Define *foreground, middle ground,* and *background.*

2. Name the four techniques you can use to create the illusion of space.

3. What is the effect of placing an object higher on the picture plane, closer to your eye level?

4. Which appears closer: an object with a greater range of values or an object with a smaller range of values?

5. Name the four basic shapes.

6. How can you keep the cones you draw from becoming lopsided?

7. How can you make a cone appear round?

8. What can you do to help you accurately draw the ellipse at the base of a cone that's lying on its side?

project

Set up a still life of cone-shaped objects on a medium-value background. Funnels and ice cream cones are obvious choices, but look also for modified cones like the bucket in this chapter's demonstration. Arrange your conical objects in various positions, setting one or two on their sides so you can practice drawing them from that angle. Be sure to establish a good, strong light source using your photoflood lamp. Take three hours to complete a charcoal drawing following the steps of this chapter's demonstration.

homework

Make four individual pencil drawings of conical objects of your choosing. Put some of the cones on their sides to practice drawing them from different angles. Don't forget to start by drawing the center guide line, adding a perpendicular line for cones that are lying on their sides. Keep the background white.

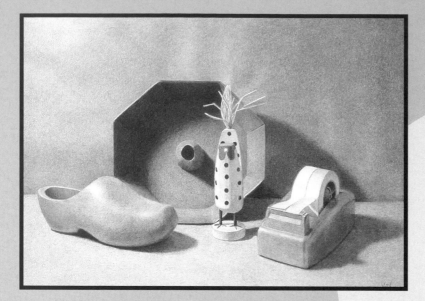

Composition and Complex Shapes

Objectives:

Understand and describe the basic principles of good composition.

Use a variety of techniques to achieve unity in a composition.

Create interest in a drawing by establishing a strong focal point.

Create symmetrically and asymmetrically balanced compositions.

Draw any complex inanimate object accurately and with a sense of volume using knowledge of the four basic shapes.

Introduction

Now that you've learned to draw all four of the basic shapes, it's time to put all your knowledge together to successfully render complex objects made up of more than one basic shape. As you train your eye in this chapter to perceive the simple shapes in complex objects, you'll also learn the principles of good composition.

COMPOSITION

A successful drawing is one that has a good composition. **Composition** is simply the overall arrangement and organization of the visual elements of your drawing on its two-dimensional surface. This chapter will use the drawings from previous chapters' illustrated demonstrations to lead you through the elements of successful composition, the key to creating a drawing that is interesting, unified, and pleasing to the eye.

Understanding Composition

Looking at a drawing or painting is like taking a visual journey. When the artist makes the journey easy and you like what you see, you are more likely to repeat the journey by looking at the drawing again and again. The works of art that hang in museums—the ones we call masterpieces—are successful in part because of their composition. The artists have so skillfully arranged, organized, and executed the visual elements in their works that they've made your visual journey effortless and pleasant, so that you're willing to take the journey again and again.

On the other hand, if the visual elements are arranged in a way that makes the journey difficult, the viewer is likely to become confused and not understand just how to look at the drawing or painting. The frustration of such an experience causes the viewer to give up on this work and go look at something else. If you look at a drawing and find yourself saying, "I don't like this," or "I don't understand what's going on here," you may be looking at a drawing that has a problem in its composition. Knowing the principles of good composition will help you invite viewers into your drawings and guide their eyes on their visual journey.

Principles of Composition

The most important compositional principles of still-life drawing are unity, focal point, and balance.

Unity

The most important principle in composition is **unity:** The viewer must see the whole first, and then the parts. When you listen to music, the first thing you hear is the song as a whole—the sum of the instruments, the voice, and the lyrics. You start to listen to the soloist only after your ear has assimilated what the whole song sounds like. The same is true in drawing. Creating unity isn't simply a matter of using objects of the same theme, such as a still life consisting entirely of fruit. What's far more interesting to the eye is a set of unrelated subjects arranged in a visually pleasing way. There could be such a thing as a band composed entirely of lead guitars, but they'd have to work hard on their arrangements to make their audience want to listen. Most bands not only have lead guitars but also basses, percussion, and singers. When a drawing has unity, the arrangement of the objects—whether they're similar or disparate—helps keep the drawing from visually falling apart. Visual unity is the first step in leading your viewer on a journey through your drawing.

One way to create unity is to place the objects in your still-life set-up close enough together that they "read" as a group rather than as unrelated individual objects. According to the **gestalt** theory of visual psychology, the human brain likes to gather information in groupings because the information is easier to process that way. You can instantly recognize a photograph as being the face of your best friend because you see all the information about your friend's face

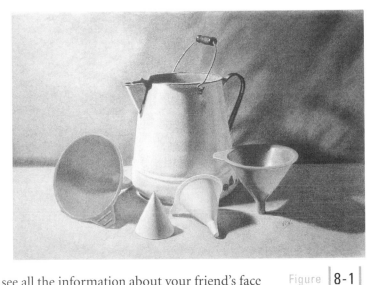

Figure | **8-1** |

in one grouping. Think how much harder it would be to recognize your friend if you saw a collection of photographs of his nose alone, his mouth alone, and one eye alone. You'd probably figure out who it is eventually, but it would take a lot longer. In Figure 8-1, the conical still-life demonstration used in Chapter 7, notice how the objects are grouped close together so that they look like one arrangement rather than a collection of individual objects. All the smaller cone-shaped objects are placed close enough to the large bucket that they overlap it. The objects "read" as one group, a still life.

Repetition is another way to create unity in your still-life arrangements. You've seen the principle of repetition in each of the illustrated demonstrations so far in this book: Every arrangement was based on just one of the four basic shapes. Figure 8-2, the still life of fruit and a bowl in Chapter 3, for instance, consists entirely of spherical shapes.

But repetition doesn't have to be quite that simple. You could choose two objects that have a sphere as their underlying structure and three that are basically rectangular, or an even greater variety of complex shapes as

Figure | **8-2** |

in Figure 8-3 and the illustrated demonstration you'll see in this chapter. A pattern of repetition, in which a particular shape is repeated, creates what is called **visual rhythm.** Visual rhythm is like rhythm in music; certain themes or melody lines or bass riffs repeat throughout the song to create the sense that this is indeed one piece of music and not just a collection of individual notes. In Figure 8-3, circles repeat throughout the drawing to unify the composition. The outer edge of the cake tin is an octagon, a shape based on the sphere. The hole in the

Figure | 8-3 |

middle of the tin is another circle. So are the dots on the wooden bird and the rolls of tape. Even the negative space of the inside of the shoe is a modified circle. The visual rhythm of this recurring pattern helps create a unified drawing.

Another aspect of repetition that unifies your drawing is your own **style or technique.** One artist might carefully blend all the gradations of tone so that they are soft and gradual throughout the drawing. Another artist might prefer to use bold blocks of tone and leave the strokes of the charcoal unblended for a more impressionistic style. Either style will result in a consistent pattern that creates unity. The problem would be if one artist combined both techniques in the same drawing. That kind of inconsistency creates confusion for the viewer and jeopardizes the unity of the whole—it looks as if two different artists drew it! There's nothing wrong with experimenting with different styles, but do it in different drawings, not in the same one. The only way to use different styles and still have one unified drawing is to create a *pattern* of inconsistency—and that's something best left to very experienced artists. When you're just starting out, stick with one consistent style for each drawing, and save your experiments in new techniques for another work.

You've already learned the importance of a strong, direct **light source** on your subject. Using just one, or at most two, sources of light also helps create unity. Look back at Figures 8-1 and 8-3. In both, the light is coming from the left and above. In Figure 8-2, the light is from the right. In all three, the light areas on each object are all on the same side of the objects, and the shadow areas are on the opposite side. The cast shadows all go in the same direction. If you use two light sources, make sure one is dominant while the other serves only as an accent. Two equally strong light sources can create confusion for the viewer, unless the artist is very experienced.

Using a single, strong light source is one way of using **continuation** as a means of unifying your drawing. Continuation establishes a clear visual path. When you extend your arm and point your finger at a distant object, your viewer looks down your arm and past the tip of your finger to find what you're pointing at. The line of your arm and finger creates a visual momentum that carries your viewer's eye to the object you want her to see. In drawing, a line—or rather, an edge, since there are no out lines in reality—is visual energy in motion. In order to go with you on the visual journey of your drawing, the viewer needs to be guided so that the eye travels along easily discerned lines or edges from one point to another until the viewer has explored the whole drawing. A strong light source, as shown in Figure 8-4, the illustrated demonstration from Chapter 2, reveals clear edges. Remember that the eye is attracted to extreme values; the more extreme the values, the easier it is to follow the edges.

The dark and light accents in Figure 8-4 establish a sort of broken visual path known as an **implied line.** An implied line is similar to a dotted line. The implied line in Figure 8-4 moves along the bottom edge of each object, from the rectangle on the left by way of its cast shadow to the dark line under the cube, where the ball picks it up and leads the eye around the bottom of the cylinder. Once the viewer has followed the implied line of the darkest values, his eye

Figure | 8-4 |

will pick up the highlights and again move across the drawing following the lightest edges on each object. This kind of continuation allows you to lead the viewer's eye wherever you choose in your drawing.

Focal Point

Another important principle of composition is creating a center of interest, or **focal point,** in your drawing to catch the viewer's eye from the very beginning. A focal point is one object or area in the drawing that is different enough from the rest to stand out visually. For instance, in Figure 8-5, the cubic still life from Chapter 4, the tissue is the focal point. It's the lightest object in the drawing, and it has an unusual shape in comparison with the cubes that make up the rest of the composition. It's possible to create a drawing with two focal points, one primary and the other secondary, but beginning artists do best to start off with only one focal point per drawing.

One technique for emphasizing an object in order to make it function as a focal point is **contrast.** In choosing objects for your still life, pick one that is clearly different from the rest. Contrast in size is one easy way to create a focal point; choose one large object among a bunch of small ones or vice versa. Contrast of shape is another option, as we saw in Figure 8-5, where the tissue is an entirely different shape from all the other objects in the drawing. If all the objects are spherical, put in one cubic object; if they're

Figure | 8-5 |

mostly cone-shaped, put in one spherical object. You can also contrast the orientation of the objects: If all the objects are oriented horizontally, choose one to place upright or on the diagonal to create a focal point. Contrast in value is another way to establish a focal point, again like the tissue in Figure 8-5, where the tissue has the lightest local value in a group of objects that are darker. Find a characteristic of one object that is different enough from the rest that the viewer will notice it first. Then further emphasize your focal point by finding as many ways as you can to contrast it with the surrounding objects.

Another way to emphasize the focal point is to draw it in greater detail than the other objects— something that is also easier if you've placed the focal point in the foreground or middle ground. If you take a photograph of your family standing in front of the Washington Monument, you focus your camera on your family's faces, not on the monument. In the resulting photograph, your family is in sharp focus with a lot of detail, while the monument is a little less clear and sharp. You want the same effect in your drawing. Take advantage of how lazy our eyes and brains are—they like to look at something that's easy to see. A sharp, clear image attracts the eye, so draw the focal point with clear edges and plenty of detail, like the bird in Figure 8-3.

How you place your focal point is crucial to the success of the composition. A good placement is near the center of the drawing, like the tissue in Figure 8-5. It's not a good idea to place it exactly dead center, which gives a kind of "bull's eye" effect. A bull's eye is not visually exciting because it's completely predictable. Instead, place your focal point *near* the center of the drawing but perhaps off a little to the left or right. Whatever you do, don't put your focal point way off to one side or the other. It will pull the viewer's eye right off to that side without giving the eye any place to go, unless you create another secondary focal point on the other side. You also shouldn't place your focal point in the background—at least, not until you have a lot of experience as an artist. You need a wide range of values in your focal point in order to attract the viewer's eye, and, as you'll remember from Chapter 6, contrast in value decreases the farther away an object is. So keep your focal point in the foreground or middle ground so that its value contrast will draw the eye.

How you choose to emphasize your focal point depends in part on the object you choose. It's probably best to start with an object that's visually interesting to begin with—the tissue rather than the cubic box it's in, the spotted bird rather than the cake tin. After that, combine as many of the techniques as you can—contrast, placement, and detail—to attract the eye and show your viewer where to begin the visual journey.

Visual Balance

Visual balance is another important principle of composition. If you drew an imaginary vertical line down the middle of your drawing to divide it in half, you should see something interesting to look at on both sides—call it "eye appeal." You need equal eye appeal to get the viewer to explore the entire drawing. If all the objects are placed on one side of the paper, why should the viewer look at the other side? Similarly, if you render an object on the right side in lots of detail with a full range of values, but there's nothing similarly rendered on the left side, the viewer's eye will be drawn to the right and not find enough reason to go to the left side.

This kind of visual imbalance is as distressing to a viewer as watching figure skaters fall in their programs at the Olympics. We'd much rather watch the skaters glide smoothly over the ice. If they fall, they get right up again and resume their program—just, for

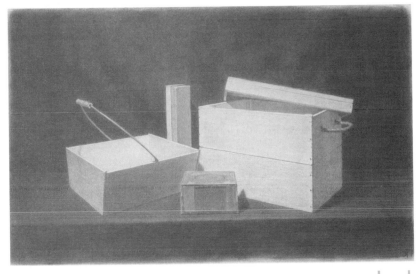

Figure | 8-6 |

that matter, as we do; if we fall, we quickly right ourselves to regain our equilibrium. Human beings love balance and hate imbalance. So when a drawing feels out of balance, it's disturbing. We look at it once or twice, and, as soon as we figure out that we can't make it balance visually, we stop looking at it. You need the sense that there's something interesting on both sides of the imaginary dividing line to keep people looking at your drawings long enough to make their visual journey. For instance, in Figure 8-6 (the still life of rectangular objects from Chapter 5), one of the two largest and lightest-colored boxes is on the left side, while the other, the box with the handle, is on the right. Each side is further balanced by other cubic shapes, each placed differently in the picture frame.

There are two basic kinds of compositional balance: **symmetrical balance** and **asymmetrical balance.** In symmetrical balance, the objects are arranged so that the imaginary vertical dividing line creates a mirror image, with the same arrangement on either side of the line. Figure 8-7 shows symmetrical balance: a bowl in the center and two oranges on either side coming away from the bowl in the same arrangement. Symmetrical balance is easier to achieve than asymmetrical

Figure | 8-7 |

balance, but not as visually exciting. Like the bull's eye effect of putting your focal point in the center, it's predictable and visually static. That's why artists more often choose asymmetrical balance.

In an asymmetrically balanced still life, the objects are arranged differently on either side of the imaginary dividing line, like the ones in Figure 8-8. Here you have the same bowl, still with fruit on either side, but there is only one apple on the left, while there are two pieces of fruit on the right. Nevertheless, the composition is pleasing to the eye because it is balanced by the **visual weight** of the objects on either side of the bowl. The size, range of values, amount of detail, and placement contribute to the visual weight of an object.

If you draw an orange and a grape with the same range of values, as in Figure 8-9, the result is unbalanced; the orange immediately draws the eye simply because it is larger and more interesting to look at with the texture on the skin. However, if you turn that grape into a bunch of grapes, as in Figure 8-10, then you've achieved visual balance. The orange and the bunch of grapes are about the same size, so they balance each other out on the page—and they're as visually interesting as the oranges. Having two different objects with equal eye appeal gives the

Figure **8-8**

Figure **8-9**

viewer more to explore. The play of light on the individual grapes creates a texture similar to the texture of the orange, thus adding to the sense of balance.

Yet it's possible to create balance among objects of unequal size by using values and detail. In Figure 8-11, the grape shows a full range of values and as much detail as you can get out of single grape. The highlight is surrounded by a much darker value than the highlight on the orange; the greater contrast draws the viewer's eye to the grape. The orange has a more gradual contrast in values, but the detail in its texture nevertheless also draws the eye. Once again, you have achieved balance, not by size but by values and detail.

Another way to achieve asymmetrical balance is in the way you place your objects. In Figure 8-8, note how the apple on the left is separated from the rest of the group. Perhaps it's not quite far enough away to have become the focal point of the drawing, but it's far enough away to draw attention to itself. Its distance from the other objects gives it a visual weight that helps balance the group of two fruits on the other side of the bowl. That apple, too, because it's in the foreground, is slightly larger than the other two fruits. Its local

Figure | 8-10 |

Figure | 8-11 |

color is also darker, and it's entirely surrounded by the white background, which increases the contrast in values.

You can combine some or all of the aspects just listed—size, value, detail, and placement—to achieve visual balance in an asymmetrical work. It takes practice to know when you have created asymmetrical balance. A good rule of thumb is simply to follow your instincts. Remember, human beings love balance and hate imbalance. If you step back and find yourself looking at only one side of your drawing, you have imbalance. If you keep going over one area, trying to add more detail and adjust the values, you're probably trying to correct an imbalance. Once again, squinting is your best friend. Compare the values on one side of your drawing to the other. Unless you're consciously doing a symmetrically balanced piece, you don't necessary want all the darks on the right side to be exactly the same as the ones on the left. But you would expect that if there's one value 10 area on one side, there will be another value 10, perhaps in a different area, on the other side. When you get to the point that you don't feel the need to adjust any more, you've probably achieved visual balance. Trust your instincts and they will serve you well.

Selecting a Viewpoint

In a drawing class, the instructor typically sets up the still-life subject for all the students to draw. So you don't have the choice in this case about which objects to include or how to place them. Nevertheless, you make decisions about the composition of your drawing the minute you set up your easel. The angle from which you view the still life determines the composition of your drawing, so that your drawing will be different from that of the student next to you or across the room. So don't just come in and set up your easel; walk all the way around the still life. You can do a successful and pleasing composition from any angle, so the question is, What interests *you* as the artist? Thinking about the angle will give you the most interesting shape for the still life as a whole. What works well as a horizontal shape from one angle may be more interesting as a vertical shape for another. From one angle, one particular object is clearly the focal point, but from another angle an entirely different object emerges with the most emphasis. Which angle gives you the most dramatic, or the most subtle, play of light and shadow as you vary the direction of the light source by walking around the subject? Choose the vantage point that interests you most and set up your easel there. If you're bored with what you're drawing, how will the viewer feel? On the other hand, if you're captivated by the composition you've chosen, you'll be able to convey that excitement to the viewer.

Particularly since you're just learning to draw, it's important to vary your vantage point in order to give yourself practice in drawing a variety of objects from a variety of angles. Don't limit yourself prematurely by learning to draw only from your favorite position in the classroom. Similarly, vary your eye level from time to time. Choose a different chair or stool than you usually use; another time draw while standing, and another time try sitting on the floor. If you're setting up still lifes at home, you can achieve a similar effect by putting something like a pile of telephone books on top of the table before putting the background cloth and then the objects on it. By raising the still-life set-up, you're lowering your eye level in relation to the subject and getting a new vantage point from which to draw.

Armed with your knowledge of the principles of composition, you're now ready to learn to draw objects that have more than one basic shape as their underlying structure.

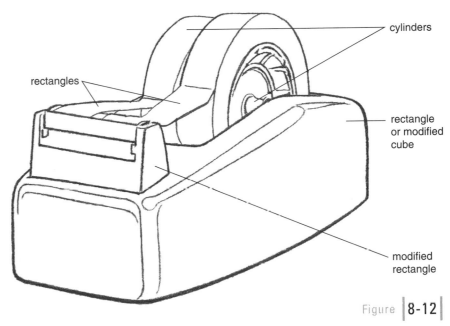

rectangles

cylinders

rectangle or modified cube

modified rectangle

Figure | **8-12** |

COMPLEX SHAPES

You've learned to draw all four basic shapes—the sphere, the cube, the cylinder, and the cone—accurately and with a sense of volume. Now you can draw complex shapes that have more than one basic shape as their underlying structure. It's simply a process of looking at an object, like the tape dispenser in Figure 8-12, not as the object itself but as a collection of basic shapes. This tape dispenser is nothing more difficult than a collection of cylinders and modified rectangles once you've learned to see it that way.

Though we focus in this book on inanimate objects in still life drawings, the same principles apply to other kinds of drawing such as figure or landscape drawing (see Chapter 13). Once you can see the basic shapes, you follow exactly the same steps you did with simpler objects: Draw the basic shape, then modify your line drawing to correspond to the object you're seeing, then give it volume, and finally draw in the detail.

Observing the Complex Form

The first thing you should do when you set out to draw a complex object like the lamp in Figure 8-13 is to look for the basic shapes. If you try to see the object in all its complexity, you're likely to be overwhelmed, and you won't draw it accurately. On the other hand, once you recognize your old friends the

Figure | **8-13** |

basic shapes, the simplification process in your brain will make it easier for you to draw it. It's a lot easier to draw a partially modified sphere, a cone with the top cut off, and some cylinders—which is all the lamp really is—than to draw the lamp as a whole.

As you observe the basic shapes, you should also, as always, observe how the light reveals the volume of the object. Where is the light coming from, and what are the lightest areas and the darkest areas? Where will you need to increase contrast in order to bring part of the object forward? Since you've already recognized the shapes in the objects, you know the answers: In a sphere, like the body of the lamp, the greatest contrast in value comes at the curve that's closest to the viewer's eye; the same is true of the cones that make up the base, stem, and shade.

Drawing Complex Objects

Once you've found the basic shapes in the complex object you're drawing, you sketch them in exactly as you did for simpler objects: a sphere and a series of cones take shape on your paper. The more complex the object, the more likely it is that your drawing will become lopsided as you add one simple shape to another. To prevent your drawing from becoming skewed, draw a central guide line. Before you begin drawing the object, determine whether its overall orientation is horizontal or vertical, and lightly draw the line in that direction.

Proportion is also important in drawing complex shapes. Be sure to measure every shape against every other shape. How high is the lampshade in relation to the sphere or the base? How wide is the base in relation to the sphere? Use sighting techniques to measure, keeping each basic shape aligned along the central guide line, and you'll end up with an accurate line drawing.

Then it's time to think in tone to give the object volume. Note the angle of the light source and squint to determine the lightest and darkest values. A complex object such as the lamp in Figure 8-14 may have more than one local color. In this case, the background is white, the shade has a light local value, and most of the values in the metal

Figure | 8-14 |

base are darker than those of the shade or the background. As you fill in first local values and then the volume revealed by the light, keep thinking in basic shapes so that you don't become overwhelmed by the complexity of the object. You may not know how to give volume to the base of a lamp, but you do know how to give volume to a sphere and a cone. Remember to use contrast in value to bring an area forward in the picture plane, but be sure to keep the value ranges of the light areas and shadow areas separate. As always, fill in the detail last. Thinking in basic shapes makes it easy to render volume in a complex object.

SUMMARY

Previous chapters taught you how to render objects accurately and with a sense of volume. In this chapter, you learned how to put individual objects together to create an interesting, unified, and balanced composition, one that invites your viewer to go on a visual journey through your drawing. You've also graduated from the four basic shapes to complex objects whose underlying structure consists of more than one shape. You're *almost* ready to draw any object you see. All that remains is to study a few special materials whose makeup presents particular challenges in drawing: drapery, metal, and glass.

Illustrated Demonstration

Complex Objects Still Life

Each of the objects in this chapter's illustrated demonstration has more than one basic shape as its underlying structure. As you follow the steps in the demonstration, pay particular attention to the way I use values to create a pleasing composition.

Step 1 | **Look.**

In looking at the still-life set-up shown below, I see four complex shapes against a medium-valued background. The focal point of this composition is the wooden bird statue: it's an unusual object to begin with, and it shows great contrast in local value between its main light color and its dark polka dots. The light is coming from the left and above. The darkest values are in the hole in the center of the cake tin and its shadow area, the spots in the shadow area of the bird, and the cast shadows directly under each object. The lightest values are in the highlights; I note that the light area of the cake tin is the inside right side. The basic shapes I see are a cylinder for the shoe, modified by the negative space for the heel of the foot and the toe. I also see a cylinder turned into an octagon with equal sides and with a modified cylinder in the center for the tube of the cake tin. I see a tall, modified cylinder for the body of the bird, long skinny cylinders for the legs, a short, squat one for its base, and a small cone for the beak. The tail is a little tricky, its mostly a cylinder for the center and each straw piece is drawn individually like detail. The tape dispenser has a rectangle for the base, cylinders for the rolls of tape, and the actual tape coming off the roll is more rectangles.

Step 2 | **Transfer the Information.**

Having positioned the still life on my paper, I begin with the largest object, the cake tin, visualizing its basic cylindrical shape and sketching that on the paper. Then I sketch each object with its underlying overall basic shape, first for position and size in relation to the cake tin and then I go back and modify each shape to look more like what I see. Beginning again with the cake tin, I'm looking directly into both the cylindrical shape of the body of the cake tin and the

tube in the center. I sight all the angles of the sides of the cake tin to modify the cylinder into an octagon, and carefully sight and measure the placement of the shape of the inside cylinder in relation to the outside shape. Once that is done, I turn to the bird; I begin by drawing a central vertical guide line, to help me keep my drawing straight, through the two cylinders I drew for position; one for the body and one for the base. I then carefully measure the distance between the upper one and the base in relation to the cake tin. After that, I draw in the legs and a cylinder for the tail. The only way to draw the stray tail pieces is to sight and measure them in relation to the cake tin and the core of the tail piece. Then I sight a circle for the cone of the beak, making sure it is positioned correctly. Moving to the cylinder for the shoe, I sight and transfer the angle along the base of the shoe. Then I can determine the top of the instep of the shoe by sighting it in relation to the cake tin. I do the same for the tip and the back of the shoe. Then I can connect the edges in between by sighting the angles. The tape dispenser comes last; using the rectangular shape, I sight carefully to determine the correct angles of the edges and I make sure I draw the dispenser in its proper two-point perspective. To accurately draw the two rolls of tape, I once again use guide lines for the center of the cylinders and the ellipses. When my

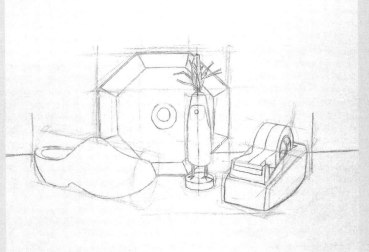

drawing has captured the correct shapes and proportions of the still life as a whole, as shown here, I'm ready to move on to the next step.

Step 3 | **Block in the Background.**

Turning my vine charcoal on its side, I fill in a darker value for the background wall and a somewhat lighter one for the tabletop, including the lines that represent the edges of the objects wherever possible. Covering up most of the paper, as shown here, will keep me from being distracted by the white of the paper when I block in tones for the local values of the objects.

Continues

Illustrated Demonstration

Continued

Step 4 | **Block in the Tones.**

I squint to see the local value of each object. The cake tin is about the same value as the background; I block in that value. What separates it from the background are the shadow areas inside and the cast shadow outside. The bird stands out against the cake tin because it is so much lighter, so there I block in only shadow areas. The shoe is a medium value, again a similar value to the wall value. I block in the shadow areas to keep it separated from the background. The tape dispenser has the same value problem as the cake tin and shoe. The body is darker

than the tabletop but the same as the wall behind. It is the value of the rolls of tape that help separate it from the wall. I block in a value for the body and only tones for the shadow areas of the rolls of tape. After that, I go back to block in the shadow areas of each object, such as the inside left of the cake tin and the right side of the tape dispenser. Finally, I block in the cast shadows of each object, carefully sighting their angles. Now my drawing is beginning to take form.

Step 5 | **Create Volume.**

As I increase the range of values to suggest the volume of each object, I want to make sure that I have a lot of contrast in the bird so that it remains the focal point of my drawing. When I add the spots in the next step, this will really make the bird stand out. To draw the tail, I switch to visualizing negative space and transfer those dark values to the tail area. The shoe and the tape dispenser are both in front of the cake tin, so I need contrast there

to bring them forward in the picture plane. I darken the shadow areas, particularly in the areas closest to the light areas, to create that contrast. Because the shadow areas of the cake tin are particularly dark, I will need the compressed charcoal to get those values dark enough to adjust the rest of the values to them. I switch back to the vine charcoal to continue creating volume in the rest of the objects. Now my drawing looks like the one shown here.

Step 6 | **Finish the Drawing.**

As I proceed to finish my drawing, I keep in mind the principles of composition that will make it a pleasing visual journey for the viewer. Implied lines along the edges of objects will help move the viewer's eye through the drawing, so I darken the background especially along the top edges of the objects to make the edges more visible. I also see I need to darken the tabletop. Next, the values in the shadow areas of the objects also need darkening to keep the separation from the background a bit stronger. I darken the cast shadows directly under each object in order not only to make the objects sit firmly on their surface but also to create another implied line along the bottoms of the objects. The highlights also will move the viewer's eye through the drawing, so I reestablish them as necessary with my kneaded eraser, especially along the edges of the cake tin.

Knowing that the bird is the focal point of the picture, I want to be sure to capture the widest possible range of values in this object. I darken the edges around it to increase the contrast. I also want to sharpen the edges, and then I add the spots, which are sure to draw the viewer's eye. The spots in the light area are slightly lighter than those in the shadow area. I add subtle gradations of tone to the tail pieces.

Finally I step back and look at my drawing. I want to make sure not only that the values are correct, but also that the composition holds together as a still life and has a sense of unity. I try to see my drawing as an impartial viewer. Where does my eye go first? I hope it's to the spotted bird, with its interesting shape and strong contrast of values. Does my eye travel comfortably along the implied lines I've established? I make an imaginary vertical line down the center and ask if my drawing, below, seems balanced. I like the way the dark shadow on the inside left of the cake tin balances the cast shadow against the wall, with interest of the spotted bird in between, and the way the shape of the shoe and the shape of the tape dispenser are arranged so that they balance each other. When I feel I've achieved a pleasing rendition of the objects I'm seeing, my drawing is finished.

things to remember

- The key to a successful drawing is a good composition that attracts the viewer's eye to a specific point and then guides the eye throughout the drawing.

- The sense that a drawing hangs together as a whole is called *unity.*

- Unity can be achieved by placing objects close enough together to read as a group; by using repetition, visual rhythm, a consistent style, and a single strong light source; and by establishing implied lines to guide the viewer's eye through the drawing.

- The *focal point* is the object in the still-life drawing that first attracts the viewer's eye.

- The focal point can be established by contrast in size, shape, or value with the other objects; by isolating it; by placing it near (but not exactly in) the center of the drawing; and by rendering it in more detail and with greater contrast in value than the other objects.

- A successful drawing must be balanced.

- Symmetrical balance is easier to achieve but less visually interesting than asymmetrical balance.

- Asymmetrical balance depends on the relative visual weight and on the placement of the objects in your composition.

- The best way to draw complex objects is to mentally break them down into the four basic shapes that make up their underlying structure.

- A center guide line is useful in keeping drawings of complex objects from becoming lopsided.

- Correct proportion is essential in accurately rendering complex objects.

in review

1. Define *composition* in still-life drawing.

2. Name the three basic principles of composition described in this chapter.

3. Why is it important to place the objects in a still-life drawing close together?

4. What is an implied line?

5. Name three ways to establish a particular object as the focal point of your drawing.

6. What is the first step in deciding whether a composition is visually balanced?

7. Name three aspects that help determine the visual weight of a drawn object.

8. Why is asymmetrical balance more visually pleasing than symmetrical balance?

9. What should you do to ensure that the complex objects you draw don't turn out lopsided?

project

In this project, you will create two compositions, choose the one that pleases you most, and create a finished charcoal drawing of that composition. Wander around your home looking for complex objects made up of more than one basic shape. Choose four or five such objects that you find visually interesting, place a cloth behind and under the objects to simplify the background, and arrange the objects on the cloth in a horizontal pattern. Choose an object for your focal point and place it in the foreground near the center of the composition. Arrange the other objects around and behind it in a way that is unified and creates a sense of balance. Step back and do a rough sketch of this composition, taking no more than half an hour to place the objects and roughly block in their values. Mark the position of each object on the cloth with charcoal or small bits of tape, because you're about to move the objects but need to be able to recapture this composition later.

Now take the same objects and create a different composition, perhaps a vertical one this time. Choose a different object to be your focal point; you might rearrange the light source to shine more strongly on this new object. Create an entirely new composition from this same group of objects, and again do a rough sketch.

Look at the two sketches and decide which one pleases you most. Finish that drawing.

homework

Choose four different complex objects and do small pencil drawings of each one individually. Remember to visualize the basic shapes that underlie the complex objects. Use a central guide line to help you keep the objects straight, and measure carefully to ensure that you achieve the correct proportions. Shade each object to give it its volume.

Drapery

Objectives:

Understand the role of drapery in the composition of a still life.

Accurately draw the form of a fold of fabric and shade it to give the illusion of volume.

Render the tones of fabrics of a variety of local colors, adding any patterns in the fabric as details.

Use patterns of light and shadow to render the textures of various kinds of fabric.

Introduction

Artists use drapery as part of their still-life compositions in order to lend interest and movement to their work. This chapter will show you how to accurately render draperies in your still-life drawings.

DRAPERY

UNDERSTANDING DRAPERY

Drapery, the artistic arrangement of fabric or clothing, has been used as still-life subject matter for centuries. Drapery can act as an important compositional device in a still-life drawing. The folds in a piece of fabric create movement that guides the viewer's eye through the drawing. The structure of the folds acts as a sort of road map, creating a visual pathway. Thus, including drapery and clothing in your still-life set-up can make for a dynamic visual experience.

The Form of a Fold

Fabric is usually fairly soft, so it takes on different shapes depending on how it's arranged. You've already dealt with fabric that has been arranged flat on a tabletop or a wall to create a

background for a still life. You've seen how light affects even a flat fabric surface—the area closer to the light is somewhat lighter than the areas that receive less light.

When something stresses the fabric, so that it does not lie flat, then folds are created. In Figure 9-1, the fabric is hanging from a pushpin. This one point of stress creates folds that hang downward without interruption due to the pull of gravity. The folds start out small at the point of stress and then get larger as they fall, so they're basically conical in shape. When there is more than one point of stress, as you'll see later, the pattern is somewhat different.

Another kind of fold is a crease, as when a fabric has been left folded for a long time or has been ironed. When such a fabric hangs from a pushpin, as in Figure 9-2, the folds have a sharp edge rather than the rounded ones you saw in Figure 9-1. While drawing a rounded fold is like drawing a cone, drawing a sharp crease is like drawing the edges of a cube or rectangle. Note how, in the foremost fold in Figure 9-2, the crease creates a sharply defined edge. The other folds are more rounded.

Volume in Folds

Drawing drapery is a study in creating the illusion of volume and space. The folds are like hills and valleys. The center of a fold comes forward toward the viewer, while the sides recede into the next fold, like a valley, and then rise again into the hill of the next fold. As with any rounded object, you create

Figure | 9-1 |

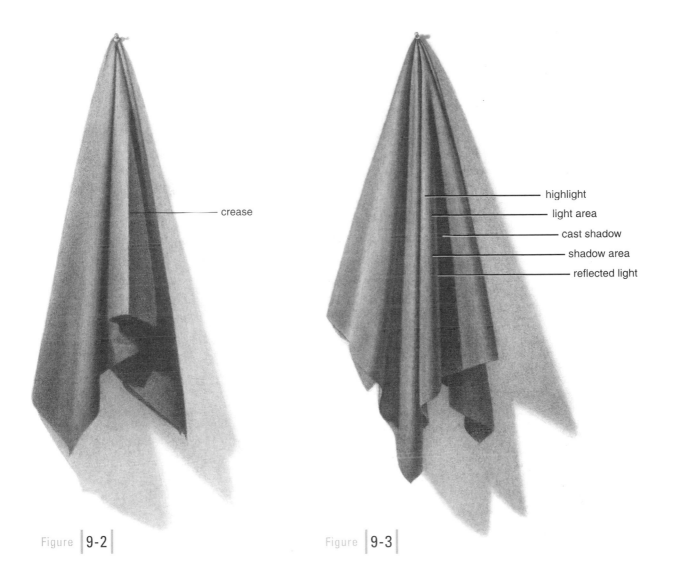

crease

highlight
light area
cast shadow
shadow area
reflected light

Figure | **9-2** |

Figure | **9-3** |

volume with contrast in values. The more contrast between the light part of the fold that comes toward the viewer and the dark part that recedes, the more volume you will create. The same is true of a fold that is a sharp crease: The more contrast in value between the forward edge of the crease and the part of the fabric behind the crease, the more the crease will appear to come toward the viewer's eye.

Observe the patterns of light and shadow areas in the drapery in Figure 9-3. The most prominent folds have a light area and a shadow area. Within the light area, there is a highlight, though it may be difficult to discern since most fabric tends to absorb rather than reflect light. The highlights are more obvious when the fabric is a shiny one like silk or some leathers. If the highlights are hard to see, look for the direction of the light source. The part of the fabric that is in a straight line with the center of the light source will be the highlight. It's important to see and render this highlight in order to give the fold its full volume.

When a fold is in the shadow of another fold, it may have only shadow areas; but, even within those shadow areas, there will be areas of reflected light. Obviously such a fold will have the appearance of less volume than one that has both light and shadow areas. Folds also have cast shadows, which are usually the darkest areas in the entire subject. There's reflected light within the cast shadow, so that even the cast shadow is not all the same dark tone. If you have trouble seeing the gradations of tone in the cast shadows of a drapery, walk up to the subject and observe it closely, and then go back to your drawing and render the subtle gradations of tone that you saw from up close.

The gradations of tone in a drawing of drapery are thus very smooth as one fold moves into the next. The more subtle gradations in tone you make, the softer and rounder the folds will appear. When the fabric is creased, the contrast between light and shadow areas is much more dramatic, as in a cube. As in any still-life drawing, be sure to keep the range of values in the light areas and shadow areas distinct from each other.

DRAWING DRAPERY

Now that you understand the form and volume of a fold, you're ready to start drawing. We'll begin with a basic piece of white fabric, learning to draw its shape and volume, and then proceed to some special cases: colored fabric, patterned fabric, and textured fabric.

Drawing the Form of Folds

In many ways, drawing the shape of a piece of drapery is similar to drawing the other objects you've learned to draw in this book, but there's an important difference: The folds of the fabric have no physical edges like those of other objects. The piece of fabric itself does have edges; if you look again at Figure 9-1, note that you can see some of the edges along the bottom of the drapery, where these edges meet the background wall. However, the edges of the fabric along the sides where the fabric meets the wall are hidden by folds, and the folds themselves have no edges because each fold merges continuously into the next.

Begin your drawing, as always, by visualizing the drapery as a whole, as one shape, and transferring that shape to the paper. To begin drawing the folds in the fabric, squint to see the basic shape of each fold. You might begin with the largest or more prominent fold, or you may choose to work from left to right or vice versa. There's no right or wrong way to draw in the folds; it's simply a matter of what makes the most sense to you based on the particular piece of drapery you're looking at. Simplify as much as you can, visualizing the basic conical shape of each fold. Use sighting techniques to capture the angles of the sides of each fold and to determine the proportions of one fold to another. Use light lines at first in case you find later that you haven't gotten the proportions of one fold to another quite right.

When drawing the bottom edge of the folds, remember that the basic shape of a fold is a cone. The edge can therefore create a modified ellipse. However, depending on how the fabric drapes, you may not see the ellipse. In Figure 9-3, the front of the bottom edge of each fold snakes into the next conical shape. Though you do have to consider your eye level in relation to the fabric, you really don't have to contend with elliptical perspective as you would with a true solid conical shape. Each fold has its own characteristics, making the shape of each bottom edge unique to each fold. The best way to render the bottom edge of a fold is to simplify the shape in your mind. If you see the entire ellipse, see that shape in proportion to the fold and the surrounding folds. If you see only the front edge, follow the pattern of the fabric around with your mind and see how the edge of that fold turns into the next fold. Then use sighting and measuring techniques to draw each part of the edge in relation to the surrounding folds.

A special trick that works well in drawing drapery is to establish landmarks to keep from becoming confused as you try to render many similar folds. The light area of the largest or most prominent fold might be your first landmark. Additional landmarks will help you determine where one fold ends and another begins. For one fold, the dark cast shadow along the edge might become the landmark that determines the beginning of this fold, while another fold's landmark is the edge where it turns into another fold. At this point, keep your drawing as simple as possible, like the line drawing in Figure 9-4. Only the most prominent landmarks have been drawn to indicate the position and shape of each fold. If your line drawing is too complex, you might become confused when you start to render the volume of the folds, perhaps blocking in a shadow on what is actually a light area.

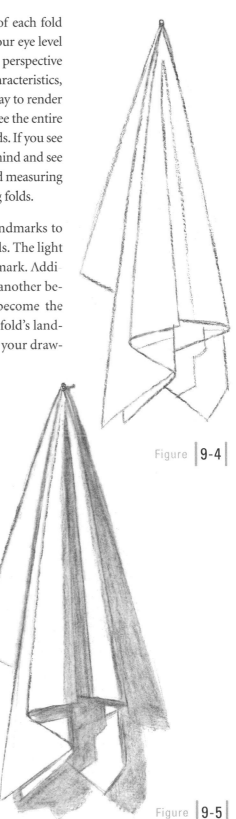

Figure | **9-4** |

Rendering the Volume of Folds

Now it's time to stop thinking in line and start thinking in tone. Squint to see the pattern of light and dark on the fabric. Recognize the largest or more obvious shadows and see them as shapes in their own right. Locate these shadow areas on your drawing and block them in right away, leaving them somewhat lighter, for now, than the actual value you see. It's easy to get lost when you try to render a lot of similar folds; if you correctly block in these first, most prominent shadow areas, you'll have started a road map that can keep you from becoming confused. If the background has its own local color, block in that value. If the fabric has a light local color, block in a tone for its cast shadows. At this point your drawing is something like Figure 9-5—it doesn't look like much of anything yet, but you've set up the landmarks that will help you render the full range of values you see in the drapery.

Figure | **9-5** |

Once you've established the large shadow patterns, start building up the values of the shadows in the folds, using your landmarks to help you find your place. You may find it useful to actually count the folds when you near the stress point that creates them, since they're so close together and narrow. Counting will keep you from merging two folds into one. Be sure to step back and squint to make sure that the shadow areas in your drawing are the same size, shape, and approximate value as the ones you see in your subject. Finally, create the illusion of the softness of the fabric by gradating the tones in your drawing. The more gradations of tone you can render, the softer your fabric will look. Use your finger or a paper stump to blend the transition from the light areas to the shadow areas. Look for the gradations of tone within the shadow areas and darken the darkest parts, leaving the original tone you blocked in as the area of reflected light. Don't let the areas of reflected light within the shadow areas get too light, or those areas will start to jump forward in the picture plane. Darken the cast shadows, gradually filling in tones until you achieve the values you see. As you work, squint frequently to compare values, and be sure to keep the range of values separate in the light, shadow, and cast shadow areas. Continue darkening and blending until you have achieved the subtle gradations that are characteristic of this piece of drapery, as shown in Figure 9-6.

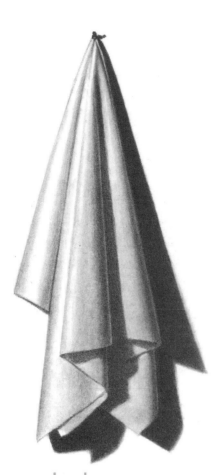

Figure 9-6

Colored Fabric

To draw a fabric that is any color other than white, you'll need to block in a tone for the local color. First, draw the outline of the outside shape of the drapery as a whole, then squint to determine the value of the local color and block in a tone for that value. Even if the local color is very dark, like the fabric on the left in Figure 9-7, you shouldn't make this initial tone too dark, because your next step is to draw lines on top of that tone to represent the shapes of the folds, and you need to be able to see those lines. Using your finger, lightly spread the charcoal around the internal area of the fabric. Don't use the paper stump for this task, because you can't afford to scrub the charcoal into the paper; later you'll need to go back to a lighter value, perhaps even the white of the paper, to represent the highlight.

After blocking in the tone of the local color, draw lines for the basic shapes of the folds on top of that tone, just as you did for a white fabric, leaving you with something like Figure 9-8. Then you can begin to fill in the shadow patterns, eventually covering up the lines with soft gradations of tone. After you darken the shadow areas, lighten the highlights with your kneaded eraser. If the dark fabric is against a light background, compare the values of the light areas of the fabric to those of the background color. If you have two draperies of different colors, as in Figure 9-7, also compare the values of the lighter drapery to those of the darker one. Compare the light areas of each

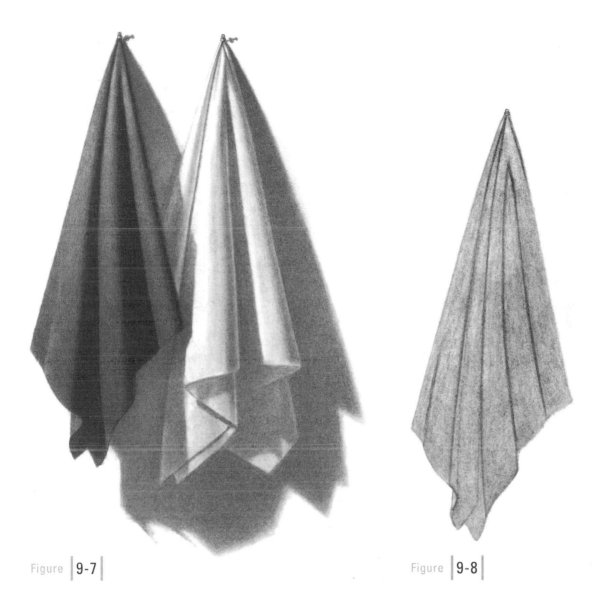

Figure | 9-7 | Figure | 9-8 |

piece of fabric, then the shadow areas of each, and then the cast shadows. The overall range of values on the darker drapery will always be darker than the overall range of the lighter drapery.

If the drapery has several stress points, creating a complicated fold pattern, you may find it easier to draw the lines of the folds before you block in the local color. This method is a little more challenging because you'll have to determine the values for each individual fold, but the advantage is that you can concentrate on the line drawing and erase lines if necessary to move or modify the shape of a fold. Make the line drawing as you would for a white fabric, and then build up tones for each section of each fold individually. As you did for white drapery, block in the shadow areas for your landmarks and then fill in the smaller shadow areas. In the light areas, you'll also build up the tones fold by fold. Keep the value ranges consistent so that all the areas "read" as the same local color.

If that method doesn't work for you, you can instead block in the tone for the local value as described and then draw on top of it, removing charcoal as necessary to represent the highlights.

Patterned Fabric

Some fabrics have patterns, like the stripes on the drapery shown in Figure 9-9. Treat such patterns as part of the structure of the fabric. Draw them in after you have established the shapes of the folds.

There are two important things to remember in rendering the detail of a pattern of stripes. The first is the shape of the stripes themselves. As a horizontal stripe flows over a fold, it creates a round line, so you will have to deal with elliptical perspective. Note where your eye level falls in relation to each stripe. If the fabric is above your eye level, horizontal stripes will curve downward; they'll curve upward if they are below your eye level. If your eye level is the middle of the whole piece of fabric, you may see some stripes curving upward and some curving downward. The horizontal stripes at your eye level will run straight across the fold.

The other thing to remember is that, while each stripe has the same local color across the entire fabric, the value of the local color will change as the stripe runs from a light area to a shadow area to a cast shadow area. If you kept the same value across the stripe, you'd flatten the form of the fold. To give a fold with a stripe pattern its volume, you must render the gradated tones of the stripe as you do for the structure of fold itself.

After you've drawn the shapes of the folds, draw in the pattern of the stripes. If the stripes are wide and of a darker value than the rest of the fabric, draw them first in line and then fill them in with a light tone for the local value. Then begin to give the folds volume with tone. Darken each value in the stripe pattern according to what you see. As you render each fold, keep in mind that the stripes are a part of the drapery and therefore have the same light source.

If the stripes are narrow and lighter than the rest of the fabric, first put a light tone down for the local value of the fabric. Don't scrub the tone in with a stump, because you may want to remove some of that charcoal. Use your kneaded eraser, molded to a point, to draw the stripe. Now render the volume of the fold, including the stripes. As you darken the

Figure | 9-9 |

shadow areas, don't lose the stripe pattern. You may have to re-establish the lighter stripes with your kneaded eraser. Squint frequently to see the values of each stripe. When you think you've finished, step back and look at the drawing as a whole to be sure that the gradations of values in the stripes still read as one local color and that they match the stripes in your subject; adjust values as necessary.

Textured Fabric

Different fabrics have different textures. So far we've dealt with fabrics that have relatively smooth textures and are not particularly reflective. However, if you wanted to draw a leather jacket like the one shown in Figure 9-10, you'd be dealing with a more reflective fabric, with distinctive patterns of light and shadow areas. Light reflects much more easily off of this kind of leather than it does, for instance, off the wool coat shown in Figure 9-11. The light areas on the leather jacket create distinct shapes with clearly defined edges, so that the transition of tones from light to dark areas is much sharper than the more gradated tones seen in the wool coat. When you begin to draw a piece of drapery, make note of the texture of the fabric. The sharper the transition of tone from light to dark areas, the more reflective the surface you're looking at. Capturing the texture of the fabric is essential to drawing drapery realistically.

SUMMARY

Imagine the interest you can add to your still-life drawings by artfully draping an attractive piece of cloth behind or over some of the objects! A piece of clothing, such as the leather jacket you saw in this chapter, can become a still-life subject in itself, perhaps paired with an object or two. If you wanted to add, say, a chain or a motorcycle wheel to go with the jacket, you'd need to know how to render the special reflective quality of metal—which is what you'll learn to do in the next chapter.

Figure | 9-10 |

Figure | 9-11 |

Illustrated Demonstration

Drapery Still Life

This illustrated demonstration will show you how to render the folds of fabric arranged in various drapery patterns, accurately drawing the folds and giving them their volume.

Step 1 | **Look.**

When I look at the still-life set-up shown here, I see three pieces of draped fabric against a flat fourth piece of fabric that serves as the background. Each has a different local value: the center drapery is white, the one on the right is very dark, and the one on the left is closer to a middle value. The background fabric is a lighter value between the values of the center fabric and the one on the left. In looking for the texture, I see that none of these fabrics have a reflective surface, because the gradation of tones between light and shadow areas is subtle and soft. I note the direction of the light source, which is from the left, and establish the value scale by noting that the lightest values are in the light areas of the white cloth and the darkest values are in the shadows of the dark fabric. I note, too, the shapes of the folds that I see. The center cloth has one point of stress and the other two on either side of it have two points of stress each. The pieces of fabric having two points of stress create a more complex pattern of folds. The major fold pattern between the stress points fall forward and downward.

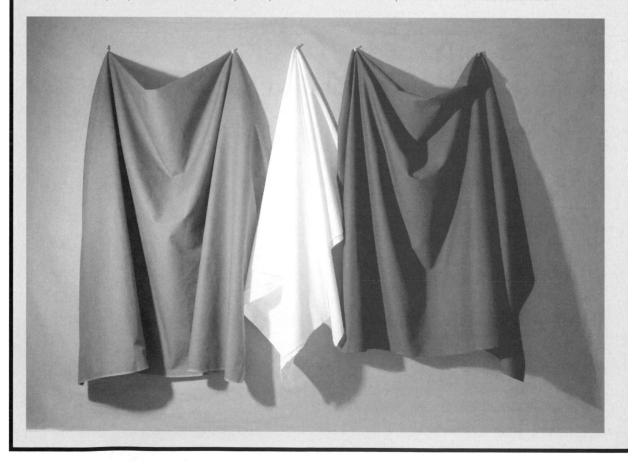

Step 2 | **Transfer the Information.**

After marking the shape of the still life as a whole on my paper, I lightly draw the shape of each piece of drapery as a whole, comparing the overall proportion of one to another. Then I turn my attention to each individual piece, beginning with the one on the left. Starting with its leftmost fold, I sight and measure to determine the angle and proportion of the fold in relation to the other folds and to the pin that holds up that side of the cloth. Since this piece has two stress points, I use the pins as a point of reference to sight and measure each fold. The major fold created between the two pins has a center point in the fold along the top edge. I measure and mark where this point lies between the pins. This fold and the one below it are upside-down cones. I transfer the angles of the top fold using the center point to help establish the apex of the cone, which is below the center point. Then I can transfer the second fold in reference to the one I've just drawn. Next, I transfer the folds to the right of the pin, using the center fold as reference. In essence, I see one large cone shape made up of smaller cones. Now I turn to the white cloth in the middle, transferring the folds in reference to the single pin and to the cloth at the left of it. Since this drapery has only one stress point, it is less complex than the other two pieces. Finally, I move to the dark cloth to the right and transfer the shape of its folds as I did for the first drapery with two stress points. I use the two pins and the two pieces of cloth I have already drawn as references. I check the negative space to make sure that I have accurately placed each drapery in relation to the one next to it. When I've finished, I have an accurate line drawing.

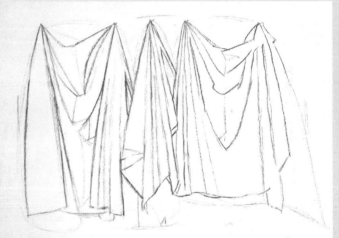

Step 3 | **Block in the Background.**

Turning my vine charcoal on its side, I block in the local value of the background fabric, including as much as I can of the outlines of the pieces of drapery in this tone and blending with my finger. Now I have white shapes against a tone for the background.

Continues

Illustrated Demonstration

Continued

Step 4 | **Block in the Tones.**

I start by blocking in tones for the local values of the two darker pieces of fabric, darker on the right and lighter on the left. I blend these tones lightly with my finger so I don't lose the line drawing; if I do lose some lines, I draw them in again to make sure I can see them over the tone. Next, I quickly block in the larger shadow areas with a flat tone, establishing my landmarks so I can always figure out which fold from the subject drapery I'm working on at any given time. The shadow areas on the central white cloth remain very light in comparison to those on the darker cloths. Then I block in the cast shadows on the background as well as the ones created by the folds on each piece of drapery. The result is a set of abstract shapes that needs the illusion of volume in order to look like pieces of fabric.

Step 5 | **Create Volume.**

Since these fabrics are not very reflective, the gradations of tone between light and dark areas will be subtle and soft, so I begin the process of giving the folds volume by blending the tones between light and dark areas with a paper stump. Then I add more charcoal to the shadow areas where they are closest to the light areas in order to increase the contrast in values. I need the greatest contrast in the folds that are closest to the viewer's eye, so that those areas will come forward in the picture plane. The original tone I blocked in for shadows now becomes the areas of reflected light. I continually blend the tones to keep the gradations subtle in order to show the softness of the folds. I look closely into the cast shadow areas to see the subtle gradations of tone that give the illusion of three dimensions and darken as much as I can with the vine charcoal. I find that the values in the dark cloth to the right are so dark that I need to use the compressed charcoal now. This will help keep this cloth looking darker than the one to the left of the white one. I also darken some of the values in the one to the left to stay consistent with the darker cloth to the right. I need to work all the values of the cloths together. As I darken one area I squint and compare it to another. It is important not to work on each cloth separately, but to work on all of them together. This way I can keep each piece looking different in value from another one. Now my drawing is taking shape.

Step 6 | **Finish the Drawing.**

At this stage of my drawing, I can fine-tune the values of each fold. I carefully blend in more charcoal to get the subtle gradations to make each fold look soft and create more volume. I use the charcoal that sticks to the stump to make the very subtle gradations of tone in the light areas on the white cloth. For the light areas on the two darker fabrics, I add more vine charcoal. I constantly squint and compare the values from fold to fold on each piece of cloth and at the same time keep an eye on the values in the other pieces. Then I make a clean point on a kneaded eraser to establish highlights, going down to the white of the paper on the white cloth and on the lightest areas of the pins. Though the highlights are small, they are there. As I adjust the values in each cloth, I find that I have to darken the cloth for the background and the cast shadows. Then I clean up my edges and step back once more and compare my drawing to my subject.

things to remember

- Drapery, the artistic arrangement of fabric or clothing, is an important compositional device that lends visual movement to a still-life drawing.

- One or more stress points in the fabric create the folds of a piece of drapery.

- Unless the fabric has been creased, the stress points create rounded, basically coned-shaped forms that fold into each other like hills and valleys.

- The softness of such rounded forms is created with subtle gradations of tone.

- Fabric that has been creased has sharp edges like those of a cubic form.

- The folds of a piece of drapery cast shadows on each other.

- When drawing a white or light-colored piece of fabric, create a basic line drawing and then block in the most obvious shadows in order to create landmarks that help you distinguish one fold from another.

- In drawing middle-value or dark pieces of fabric, squint to determine the value of the local color and block in a light tone before making the line drawing to represent individual folds. Alternatively, you can start with a line drawing and then block in the light and shadow areas of each fold.

- Treat any pattern in the fabric as part of the fabric; draw it after establishing the shape of the fabric as a whole.

- In drawing patterned fabric, pay close attention to the shape of the pattern as it moves over the fold and note the variations in the local color of the pattern as it travels from the light to shadow areas of the fold.

- Note the texture of the fabric you're drawing. A reflective texture shows sharp edges between light and shadow areas, while a less reflective texture shows subtle gradations between light and shadow areas.

in review

1. Define *drapery*.

2. What is the function of drapery in a still-life composition?

3. Which of the basic shapes is created by hanging fabric that has not been creased?

4. Which of the basic shapes is created by creased fabric?

5. What is the recommended way to begin a drawing of a dark piece of drapery, after establishing the basic shape of the piece of fabric as a whole?

6. How can you tell if the texture of the fabric you're looking at is reflective?

7. At what point in your drawing should you render any pattern in the fabric?

project

For your own charcoal drawing, combine what you've learned in this chapter about drawing drapery with your knowledge of how to render complex objects. Choose one to three complex objects and two pieces of cloth (in addition to the usual background cloth) of contrasting local colors. Experiment with the composition of the cloth in relation to the objects. You might pin a piece of cloth to the wall, hang it on a wire hanger, or even drape it over one of the objects. Set up your photoflood lamp well off to one side to give the most dramatic pattern of light and dark on the drapery. Once you're satisfied with your composition, take three hours to complete the drawing.

homework

Using your pencil and cold-press paper, practice rendering the volume of folds by making four drawings, each featuring one article of clothing. Arrange each piece of clothing in a different way; for instance, hang one on a hanger, drape another over a doorknob, fold another neatly, and toss the fourth gently on a table to see how it falls.

Metal

10

Objectives:

Understand the distinctive characteristics of light on highly reflective surfaces such as polished metal.

Accurately render the reflections in highly reflective surfaces with the correct range of values.

Draw flares in the highlights of metal surfaces.

Introduction

In this chapter you'll learn several techniques that will help you draw objects with highly reflective surfaces. The best example of such surfaces is polished metal. You'll learn how to render the reflections in the surface of the metal without becoming confused by the mass of information such reflections can present.

UNDERSTANDING HIGHLY REFLECTIVE SURFACES

Drawing highly reflective surfaces can be intimidating at first because there is so much to see. When you look at an object with a polished surface, you see not only the object itself in all its volume but also the reflections of whatever objects surround the object. Nevertheless, if you follow the advice in this chapter, you'll be able not only to draw objects with highly reflective surfaces but also to have fun doing it! A little game called "find the picture in the picture" will help you sort out what you're seeing. Just as you learned to find the four basic shapes in complex objects, so finding the picture in the picture will start a simplification process in your brain that will enable you to render what you're seeing.

How Metal Reflects Light

There are many kinds of highly reflective surfaces, but polished metal is perhaps the best example. The still-life drawing in Figure 10-1 shows all the characteristics of highly reflective surfaces that make them both challenging and fun to draw. Remember that the light bouncing off the surface of an object is what reveals the object's form. The surfaces of the objects you've been drawing so far in this book have not been highly reflective; rather, they absorb and diffuse most of the light that hits them, so that their form is revealed through subtle gradations of tone. The polished surfaces of the pots in Figure 10-1, on the other hand, absorb very little of the light that hits them, so that most of the light bounces right back off. This includes not only the light that comes directly from the light source, but also the light

that is bouncing off (and revealing the form of) the objects around the pots. That's what causes these objects to be reflected in the surface of the pots. You've seen that less reflective objects also catch light from the objects surrounding them, and you've been drawing, for instance, areas of reflected light within shadow areas on such objects. The difference is that the less reflective surfaces absorb and diffuse more of the light that hits them than do highly reflective surfaces such as metal. It's only in the highly reflective surfaces, then, that you can actually see a mirror image of the sur-

Figure | 10-1 |

rounding objects. These distinct reflections, with their sharp edges, are the unique characteristic of highly reflective surfaces.

Find the Picture in the Picture

The biggest challenge in drawing metal surfaces is the reflections, which can easily confuse your eye and your brain so that you can't sort out what you're seeing. That's where the game called "find the picture in the picture" comes in handy. Every shape you see in a metal surface is a reflection of some object near the metal object. Figure 10-2 shows the larger pot from Figure 10-1, with the reflections labeled so you can see how the shapes on the surface of the pot make sense when you see what they are reflections *of*. When drawing a highly reflective object, look at each of the objects around it, and then locate the reflection of each one in the polished surface. That's how you play the game of "find the picture in the picture." Because the surface of the pot is curved, the reflections are distorted, like the reflections in a fun house mirror. The degree of distortion depends on the curvature of the surface. This pot's surface is a convex curve, so, for instance, the short pot on the left appears much longer and thinner in the reflection than it is in reality. A concave curve would produce a shorter, fatter pot. The vertical lines in the reflections remain straight and vertical, but the horizontal lines have all curved due to the curvature of the pot. Note how the edges of the table also appear to curve upward in the reflection.

It's useful to identify the objects that you're seeing reflected in a metal surface, because knowing what they are can help you simplify their reflections so that you can draw them more easily. If you can't tell what a particular reflection actually is because only part of an object is reflected, identify it by color: Fix the color of the reflection in your mind and then look around the environment to find something of that color. However, when you start to draw the reflections in the metal pot, be sure to draw what you see rather than what you know. You *know* that the tabletop is flat, but the reflection you *see* is curved.

flares

reflection of
peppermill

reflection of
small pot

reflection of
table

reflections from
other side of room

reflection of
pitcher

reflection of
saucepan

Figure |10-2|

Distinct Edges

Highly polished surfaces create reflections with sharp, distinct edges. Any reflections on less reflective surfaces such as wood or ceramic are soft and diffuse, so that you render them in gradated tones. The distinct edges of the reflections are the single most important characteristic that separates metal and other highly reflective surfaces from less reflective surfaces.

Sometimes, however, the very nature of what's being reflected makes it difficult to show the sharp edges of the reflection. For instance, the lid of the pot in Figure 10-2 is reflecting the ceiling. You can't see the edges of the ceiling in the reflection, so the entire reflection appears gradated, without any sharp edges except along the rim of the lid. That's a problem. Without sharp edges, there's nothing to tell the viewer, "This is a metal surface."

Luckily, in this as in almost any metallic subject you draw, you can find details that do have sharp edges and therefore demonstrate that the surface is reflective. You need to train your eye to pick out such details in order to render a surface that "reads" as metallic. Near the center of the lid of the pot in Figure 10-2, you can see two distinct reflections with sharp edges: the light source and the knob of the lid. Rendering such details with their sharp edges will give the lid its shiny appearance despite the diffused nature of the rest of the reflection. Note, too, that as the lid curves down to fit into the pot, the curvature gives the opportunity for more reflections. Those reflections are very small, because the area of curvature is small, but it's important to render these tiny reflections in order to show that the surface is polished.

DRAWING HIGHLY REFLECTIVE SURFACES

When you start to draw a metal surface like the large pot in Figure 10-1, begin by establishing the form of the pot itself without being distracted by the reflections in the surface. As with any object, you must create the illusion of volume by applying gradations of tone. Begin by finding the direction of the light source. Establish your value scale by finding the lightest area—the highlight—and the darkest area, in this case the knob and the reflection of the peppermill. The body of the saucepan and large pot in Figure 10-1 are cylinders and the lids are modified cones that taper slightly upward toward the knobs. You'll have to use elliptical perspective to draw these shapes correctly. All of these shapes are basically round. Even though they have many reflections, you still have to give them their roundness by establishing the greatest contrast in value in the area closest to the viewer. With all those reflections, you may have only the cast shadows on the table and between the lid and the rim of the pot with which to establish this contrast.

Drawing Reflections

When you've established the overall shape of the pot, you're ready to tackle the reflections. See each reflection as a shape and break it down into one or more of the four basic shapes. Measure the angles and proportions of the reflections exactly as you would any other object. You're drawing a picture within a picture.

The light from reflected objects will always be darker in value than the light from the direct light source. The variation in value created by the reflected objects may mean that the ranges of values in a drawing of a metal surface may not be as distinct as they are in a drawing of less reflective surfaces; that is, you may find that the range of values in the light area actually overlaps the range in the shadow area because of the reflections in the light area. Nevertheless, you must establish a separate, *overall* range between light and shadow areas in order to give the metal object its volume.

Remember that the edges of the reflections in a metal surface must be sharp and distinct. When you have an area that reflects one large area with no edges, like the lid of the pot, be sure to look for and render the small details that do have sharp edges in order to clearly show that the surface is metallic.

Drawing Flares

Another unique characteristic of highly reflective surfaces is the **flare.** When an intense direct light hits a highly polished surface, it can create a starburst effect at the highlight. This sparkle immediately says "metal" to the viewer.

Create the flare in your highlight as part of the detail work, toward the end of the drawing. You'll be tempted to overwork the flare so that it looks labored and loses its effervescence. The effect you're after, though, is simplicity that looks as if it happened without effort. It's difficult to remove an unsuccessful flare. Thus, it's a good idea to practice your flare on another piece of paper before attempting it on your drawing.

Start by making sure that your highlight is the white of the paper and has defined edges. Then take your kneaded eraser and make as fine a point as you can with it. Start at the center of the highlight and stroke upward to make one arm of the flare. Reroll your eraser so you have a clean point, and, again starting at the center, stroke downward to make the other vertical arm. If the flare is intense enough, repeat to make two horizontal arms. Then, if the flare is really intense, draw the diagonal arms somewhat shorter than the horizontal and vertical ones, as shown in Figure 10-3. Now

Figure | **10-3**

stop. If you go back to try to rework the flare, you're likely to overwork it instead. It's better to leave it as an imperfect flare than to produce a labored effect.

SUMMARY

Drawing metallic objects creates special challenges for any artist because it's easy to be confused by the reflections in a highly reflective surface. Yet if you follow the advice in this chapter, you'll be able to draw any metallic object with confidence. Remember to draw the form of the basic metal object before you even start to think about reflections. When you turn to the reflections, find the "picture in the picture" and draw it exactly as you see it, remembering that the value of reflected light is always darker than the value of direct light. Draw the distinct edges that are the unique characteristic of reflections in highly polished surfaces, add a simple, spontaneous flare—and voilà, you've drawn a metallic surface! You'll use similar techniques, plus a few new ones, in the next chapter to help you draw glass objects.

Illustrated Demonstration

Metallic Objects Still Life

This illustrated demonstration includes objects with varying reflectivity. There are two metallic surfaces, including one that is highly polished, as well as objects whose surfaces are less reflective and therefore produce more gradated values. Pay attention, as the demonstration proceeds, to the way in which I build up my values to create the appearance of each type of surface.

Step 1 | **Look.**

In my subject, I see a variety of objects, some with metal surfaces, on a middle-valued background. The darkest local value is the peppermill; the lightest is the pitcher. The lightest values, as usual, are in the highlights, and the darkest are in the cast shadows, in the shadow area of the peppermill, and in the black knobs and handles of the pots. The light comes from the left and above.

Two of the pots are metallic. I can see clear reflections of all the surrounding objects in the large pot in the center. The pot on the right is not reflecting as many objects. The pot on the left, by contrast, has a glossy ceramic surface, so that the only clear reflection is that of the light source. The highlights on the two pots with metal surfaces have flares.

Continues

Illustrated Demonstration

Continued

Step 2 | **Transfer the Information.**

Having placed the still life as a whole on my paper, I begin with the pot in the center. This way I can draw all the other objects in reference to it. I visualize each object as a basic shape or a combination of basic shapes and sketch in those shapes on my paper. The pots are simple cylinders and the lids have conical shapes for their underlying structures. The peppermill is a cylinder shape as well. I make note of where my eye level is so I can draw the ellipses correctly for each object. I also draw light guidelines for these ellipses. I draw a central guideline for the peppermill to keep it from going lopsided. I use guidelines to align the knobs in the centers of their lids as well. After each basic

shape is drawn for each object, I can go back and refine each shape to make it look like the object. I draw each object carefully in relation to each other object and constantly measure the proportions and align the angles. When I think I have an accurate line drawing, as shown here, I step back to make sure that it matches my subject. Note that I have made no attempt in this step to render the texture of the metallic surfaces; I won't even begin that process until I block in the tones. However, I do want to draw in the reflections of the objects on the pot in the center. I draw them in as if there were more objects in the still life. They are drawn in relation to the rest of the objects and to the pot.

Step 3 | **Block in the Background.**

As usual, I block in values for the background and the tabletop, as shown here. I'm careful not to make these medium values too dark at this stage; I will adjust the values later.

Step 4 | **Block in the Tones.**

Before blocking in tones for local values, I isolate the highlights in the reflective objects by drawing a light line around them. To make sure that metal has that "sparkle," I need to keep my highlights pure white. I also block in tones for the reflections in the center pot. I transfer each reflected object, creating a "picture in the picture," essentially a distorted image of the same still life I'm drawing. Then I can block in the tone for each background area and object in the reflection. Look how just by blocking in simple tones of the reflections, my pots are already beginning to look like they have a shiny metallic surface. All of these reflections are by their nature darker in value than the highlight, which is the reflection of the direct light

source. I draw the more diffuse reflections in the pot on the right in the same way, seeing each as a shape. Then I go back to the objects themselves and create the shadow areas and cast shadows, as usual. I stand back from my drawing and compare it with my subject.

Step 5 | **Create Volume.**

As I work to create volume, I can't let the reflections in the metallic pots distract me from the fact that those pots are not only reflective but also round. In order to make the centers of the pots come forward in the picture frame, I have to render greater contrast in value in the reflections that are toward the center of the pot and less contrast in the reflections that are on the sides, farther from the viewer's eye. The metallic pot to the right has a light reflection in the middle, yet this is the part that is closer to the viewer. I still have to bring this part forward in the picture plane. I can still do this by contrasting the values in the center of the pot with the darker values at

the edges of the pot. Also notice how the values at the edges are close in value to the background. Also, no matter how light a value might appear in one of the reflections, it can never get as light as the highlight. The pot in the center is now becoming the focal point of my drawing because the variety of values of the reflections will catch the viewer's eye first. In order to get the dark values on the peppermill, handles, and knobs, I have to use a little of the compressed charcoal at this stage. Also, there are several dark reflections that need to be dark, so I add some compressed charcoal there as well. I adjust values in every area, squinting frequently both at the subject and at the drawing.

Continues

Illustrated Demonstration

Continued

Step 6 | **Finish the Drawing.**

When I again pick up my compressed charcoal to add to the dark end of the value scale, I remind myself of the darkest values in the still life as a whole and constantly compare other values to the darkest ones so that the drawing doesn't get too dark. I also consider the balance of my composition, ensuring that there are equally dark values on either side of an imaginary vertical line down the center. The dark cast shadows on the bottoms of the objects also create an implied line for the viewer's eye to follow, as well as seating the objects firmly on the table.

I want to create the same kind of balance in the light areas, so I lighten any areas that have gotten too dark and reestablish highlights as necessary with my kneaded eraser. After the values look right, I turn my attention to the details. I need a charcoal pencil for some of the detail of the reflections because I can't get a fine enough point with either charcoal. After adjusting the values in the background, I draw in the last detail, the flares on the two metallic pots. I make a clean point on my kneaded eraser to draw the arms of the flare from the center of the highlight. These flares on the rim of the pots have distorted starbursts. The one on the reflection of the ceramic pot, for instance, has only vertical arms. I draw what I see even though I don't see a complete starburst. I tell myself I have only one swipe each way to make the flare. I have to live with the way it comes out, so I don't overwork it. When all my values are correct, my drawing is finished, as shown here, so I spray it with fixative.

things to remember

- Objects with highly polished surfaces, such as metal, reflect the objects that surround them.

- The characteristic that creates the illusion of a highly reflective surface is that the reflections have distinct, sharp edges.

- Reflected light, even in a reflection on a metal surface, is always darker in value than direct light.

- Identify the reflections in a shiny surface by looking at the surrounding objects.

- Drawing reflections is like drawing a "picture in the picture."

- If a reflection consists mostly of a large area of gradated tone, look closely for tiny reflections that have sharp edges in order to create the illusion of a highly reflective surface.

- Use shading to render the volume of the underlying structure of the object, and don't let the reflections distract you from this underlying structure.

- Flares, another characteristic of highly reflective surfaces, are created quickly and simply using a kneaded eraser.

in review

1. What is the difference in appearance between the reflections of surrounding objects in highly polished and less reflective surfaces?

2. What is the difference between the way light reacts when it hits a polished surface and when it hits a dull surface?

3. What happens to the reflections of objects on a curved surface?

4. What is the point of looking at the actual objects that are being reflected in a shiny surface as well as at the reflections?

5. What is the name for the starburst effect in the highlights of reflective surfaces?

6. What is the greatest concern in drawing such a starburst?

7. Why must the values in the reflections you draw always be darker than the highlights of the reflective object?

project

Take an inventory of the metallic objects available to you and pick one with a highly polished surface and another that is partially reflective. The kitchen is a good place to look; besides pots and pans you may also have metal bowls and utensils. You may also be able to find other metallic objects—boxes, picture frames, large chains—throughout your home. Once you've found one highly reflective surface and one that's somewhat reflective, pick out two other objects with dull surfaces. For variety, pick out another object—say a ceramic plate or mug—that is slightly reflective. Using your knowledge of the principles of composition, arrange the objects in a pleasing way, and then take three hours to complete a charcoal drawing on 18 × 24 newsprint.

homework

Take out your graphite pencils and practice drawing four individual objects with highly reflective surfaces that you can find in your home. Don't forget to give each object its volume as well as rendering the reflections.

notes

Glass

Objectives:

Understand and explain the unique properties of glass as a still-life subject.

Draw clear glass objects accurately by rendering their shape and interior reflections, any objects seen through the glass, and any objects reflected in the glass.

Draw colored glass objects with their proper local color and the shading that gives them volume.

Draw clear and opaque or translucent liquids held in a glass object, accurately rendering the way such liquids transmit or reflect surrounding objects.

Introduction

In this chapter, you'll learn how to draw transparent objects such as those made of glass. Glass objects look complicated at first glance—you can see through the glass to objects behind, which are usually distorted by the glass. You can also see reflections in the glass, any liquid that's in the glass object, and the glass's own form with its own highlights and shadows. Yet the process of drawing a glass object begins with the same principles you've learned throughout this book: seeing the basic shapes and the values of your subject and then rendering them on paper.

CLEAR GLASS

Objects you can see through, such as those made of glass and other transparent materials, offer their own set of challenges for the beginning artist, but in reality drawing a glass object is no harder than drawing any other subject. You just have to understand what you're seeing. We'll start with clear glass, the most basic kind of transparent material, and then study how to draw colored glass and glass objects containing liquid.

You begin a drawing of a glass object by drawing its shape, just as if it were solid. You break any complex object down into its basic shapes, sketch them in, and then modify them to match the object you're looking at. For instance, the wine glass in Figure 11-1 consists of a modified cylinder for the bowl of the glass plus two cones and a sphere for the stem. Because it's a complex shape, a central guide line helps in keeping the shapes together without letting the object as a whole get lopsided.

Understanding Clear Glass

Once you've captured the basic shape, it's time to render the volume of the glass. Now the transparency of the material comes into play. You can see three things that are unique to transparent materials: the thickness of the glass itself, objects seen through the glass from behind, and reflections of surrounding objects on the surface of the glass.

Seeing the Thickness of Glass

Most of the glass objects you draw, such as bottles or glasses, have an inside and an outside. You've drawn objects that had insides as well as outsides before, but only with transparent objects do you have to deal with the fact that you can see the inside as well as the outside. Note how the light, which comes from above and slightly to the left, reveals the volume of the wine glass in Figure 11-2. In some ways, the glass reacts like any solid object. For instance, the lip of the glass has its own light and shadow areas as well as a highlight at the point directly opposite the center of the light source.

However, the light also penetrates to the inside of the glass, so that there's another highlight inside the bowl of the glass at the bottom and on the base. These highlights are made by the direct light source, so that they appear as intense as the highlight on the lip of the glass. All the

Figure **11-1**

other highlights you see, like the one in the inside center of the bowl, are actually reflections of direct highlights. Since they're not caused by the light source but by a reflection of the light source, they are not as bright as the direct highlights. Some highlights appear within the thickness of the glass rather than on the surface, and some may come not from the direct light source but from another light source, such as light coming through a window. It doesn't matter if you can't identify the source of the light that's causing a highlight, as long as you can see the highlight as a shape and accurately depict its value in relation to the other values you see.

The inside of the bowl also has its light and shadow areas, as well as some reflected light. The wine glass also has a cast shadow. When the glass is clear and empty, the shadow may not appear as a solid shape. In the cast shadow shown in Figure 11-2, some parts of the cast shadow are dark but some are much lighter in value, where the light shines through the glass. Accurately drawing the values you see in a glass object will not only give it its volume but also clearly show the transparency of the material.

Figure | 11-2 |

Seeing Through Glass

Since glass is transparent, you can see through it to whatever is behind. After all, that's why windows are made of glass! However, the glass objects in still-life drawings are rarely straight and flat like window glass. More likely you'll be looking at a glass or a bottle with a curved surface. The curvature of the glass will distort the image of whatever objects are behind the glass. Figure 11-3 shows a wine glass with a candlestick behind it. Note how the curvature of the glass distorts part of the appearance of the candlestick. The distortion is greatest at the edges, where the curve is greatest. The candlestick appears less distorted in the center of the glass, though even here the wine glass is still somewhat curved. When the glass object has designs cut into it, as in the stem of the glass in Figure 11-3, the distortion is even more marked. If you're confused

Figure | 11-3 |

by what you see through the glass, you may want to take a look at the object behind it in order to understand what you are seeing.

Seeing Reflections in Glass

Besides being transparent, glass also reflects light. Though the surface of glass is rarely as reflective as that of polished metal, if the glass object is clean and well polished, you can see all sorts of reflections from other objects nearby. Figure 11-4 shows the same wine glass as Figure 11-3 with the same candlestick behind it, but now a black vase placed near the glass makes a dark reflection in the glass. As with metal, the curvature of the glass distorts the appearance of the object being reflected.

Drawing Clear Glass Objects

You can see a lot of different shapes in a glass object—the glass itself, inside and out; the objects behind the glass, and the objects reflected in the glass. In order to draw a glass object in all its complexity, you need to simplify it. See each of the light areas and shadow areas, each of the parts of the objects behind the glass, each of the reflections, as a shape in its own right, and then draw each shape you see. Then turn to rendering the volume, constantly squinting to compare values. You'll need to compare the shapes of the values you see within the glass to the values surrounding the glass. In order to give the illusion that the viewer is looking through the glass to an object behind it, you have to repeat some of the values you see next to or through the glass in the glass itself. As always, the contrast of values is what gives your glass object its volume, and the areas of greatest contrast must be those closest to the viewer's eye.

In the process of rendering the values of transparent objects, step back frequently. Up close, your drawing will not look like a glass object right away; it will have the feel of a collection of abstract shapes of various values. From farther away, it will look more "glass-like." As the drawing progresses, as you match its values more and more closely to the ones you're seeing, as you add the reflections and highlights, your glass will take form on the paper and begin to look more and more like what you're seeing.

Figure | 11-4 |

COLORED GLASS

Drawing an object made of colored glass, like the wine bottle in Figure 11-5, is similar to drawing a clear glass object. The difference is that you have to render the value of the local color. The green of the wine bottle in Figure 11-5 is about a value 5 on a scale of 1–10. This value will affect the values of any object you can see through the glass; the values of the object seen through the glass will be darker than the values of the actual object. In effect, you're seeing the values of the object through a filter of value 5, as if you were looking through a pair of sunglasses.

It's important to keep the values of everything that can be seen through the colored glass consistent, so that all the values "read" as coming through glass of the same color. The easiest way to do this is to lay down a light tone over the whole wine bottle after you've drawn its basic shape. Remember to leave the white of the paper for the highlight, but otherwise cover the whole wine bottle with a light tone to represent the local value of the green glass. Then draw in the shapes of whatever you can see through the glass. To fill in the values of those objects, begin with the lightest local value you can see through the glass. This value remains the original tone you blocked in. From there, darken the values for the rest of the shapes you can see through the glass, squinting frequently to compare values. Colored glass is reflective just like clear glass, so you'll also have to deal with reflections. Use your kneaded eraser to lighten the shapes of the reflections, but don't go down to the white of the paper or you will have drawn a highlight instead of a reflection. Don't forget that there may be other highlights from other light sources in the room other than the direct light source. For instance, in Figure 11-5, there's such a secondary highlight from another light source on the right shoulder of the wine bottle.

Figure | **11-5** |

LIQUID IN A GLASS OBJECT

Glass objects—glasses, bottles, vases, and the like—often contain liquids such as water, wine, or milk. The liquid may seem to complicate things still further, but drawing glass objects that contain liquid is still simply a matter of understanding what you are seeing. Drawing transparent or semitransparent liquids offers different challenges from drawing opaque liquids.

Transparent Liquids

When a clear glass object contains water, like the vase shown in Figure 11-6, both the object and the liquid are fully transparent—you can see right through them to what is behind or inside the vase. The difference between a vase

Figure | **11-6** |

with water in it and an empty vase is that the water can both magnify and distort the image you see through it. Note, in Figure 11-6, how the stem of the rose in the water appears to have shifted a little to the left of the rest of the stem above the surface of the water. As with an empty glass object, the curvature of the glass also distorts the shapes of objects seen through the glass.

Water is a substance and has form and volume, with its own highlights, light areas, and shadow areas. However, because water is clear and transparent, these areas are not as well defined as in a solid form. The light reveals the form of the water. In Figure 11-6, the top surface of the water is the light area, and the shadow area is below the surface. However, in this case parts of the top surface are darker than the water below it because the surface is reflective. The darker areas are reflections of the shadows of the leaves of the rose. You can also see highlights in Figure 11-6 along the front edge of the surface of the water, as well as highlights at the bottom, inside the vase. You may find it helpful to look around and behind the vase and its water to identify the objects that are being reflected.

Begin a drawing of a glass object containing transparent liquid in the same way as you would a drawing of an empty glass object, by drawing the shape of the object. Then, when it's time to give the glass object and the liquid their volume, draw the shapes of the objects you see through or reflected in the glass. Block in the most obvious tones first, and then gradually build up the values until they match what you are seeing, keeping the white of the paper for the highlights. The values of what you can see through the glass and liquid may not be the same as those of the object itself. Though the values of what you can see through a clear liquid such as water will be similar to those of the actual object, a colored, semitransparent liquid such as wine will darken the values just as colored glass does. If the liquid you're drawing is colored, start, as you did with colored glass, by laying down a light tone to represent the value of the local color, and then build the values of what you can see through the liquid on top of that tone.

Figure | 11-7 |

Opaque Liquids

If the liquid in a glass object is not transparent, then it behaves more like a solid object because you can't see through it—at least not entirely. The milk shown in Figure 11-7 is virtually, but not quite, opaque; it's very slightly translucent so that light penetrates slightly through it. The same would be true of most other non-transparent liquids such as orange juice. However, for the most part this milk acts like a solid object. You don't have to worry about seeing any objects through the milk, you can see only through the top of the glass above the milk and through the thick glass at the base of the glass. However, if there are reflections on the glass containing the milk, they will become more prominent because they're not competing with anything seen from behind the milk. In Figure 11-7, there's also a cast shadow on the surface of the milk made by the rim of the glass.

What the light reveals on this glass of milk is that the surface of the milk is the light area and the side is the shadow area. The highlight is along the back edge of the surface. The slight translucence of the milk comes into play with a slightly lighter area on the left of the shadow area. Drawing an opaque liquid is actually easier than drawing a transparent one; all you have to do is make a gradated tone in light and shadow areas and add any reflections you might see in the glass. If the liquid is something darker than milk, such as orange juice, lay down a tone to represent the value of the local color as you would for any solid object.

SUMMARY

The most important thing to remember in drawing glass objects is to understand and simplify what you are seeing. While there's a lot to see in a glass object—including the interior of the glass itself, the objects behind it, reflections, and any liquid in the glass—the key is to see each value as a separate shape and render the shape and tone as you see them. With this chapter, your course in basic still-life drawing is completed. In the next two chapters, you'll expand your horizons by learning about other drawing media besides charcoal and pencil and by exploring figure and landscape drawing.

Illustrated Demonstration

Glass Objects Still Life

This illustrated demonstration will show you how to draw glass objects containing liquids. Inclusion of a rose in this composition will give you practice in drawing objects seen through a clear liquid and introduce you to the drawing of organic objects.

Step 1 | **Look.**

In the photograph shown here, I see three glass objects, a rose, and a small white sculpture of a cat against a middle-valued background. All of the objects are complex shapes except the vase, which is a simple cylinder. The vase is made of clear glass and contains water as well as the rose. The wine glass is also clear and contains red wine. The bottle, which is green glass, also contains some wine. The light comes from the left and above; I can see an image of the light source in the highlights on the shoulder of the wine bottle. The highlights and the cast shadows directly under the objects establish the extremes of my value scale. The wine bottle and wine in the glass are my darker objects; the cat is the lightest. The rose will be the focal point of my drawing because it is different from the other objects and so stands out visually. The light is strongest on the rose, creating a wide range of values from dark to light. The rose is a complex organic shape while the others are artificial and simpler. The rose stands at an angle, creating a directional line to guide the eye through the drawing, while the other objects stand upright. In addition, the surface texture of the rose is different from the smooth, reflective surface of the remaining objects.

Step 2 | **Transfer the Information.**

The height of the rose makes this still life a vertical composition, so I turn my pad vertically and mark the shape of the whole composition, as usual. I lightly position the objects by drawing each one in turn with their underlying basic shape. Once each shape is proportional to the object and in relation to each other, I modify these shapes into the objects. At first, I ignore the liquid so that I can capture the shape of each object. The wine glass and the bottle, as complex shapes, need a center vertical guide line to help line up the smaller basic shapes. For the rose, I sight to determine the angle of the stem and the positions of the leaves and the flower, also in relation to the other objects. When drawing an organic object it is important to really see the basic shapes that make up the overall object. It is easy to get lost in the detail of the shape and lose the proportions. I draw basic shapes—a cylinder for the main part of the flower and cones, spheres, and rectangles for the leaves—and then modify them to look more like the flower and leaves I'm seeing. As always, I sight and measure to determine that the objects are correctly positioned and in proportion to each other, visualizing the negative space as necessary.

Only when I have captured the shapes of the objects do I turn to the liquids, drawing ellipses for the surfaces of the water in the vase and the wine in the glass. I see the part of the rose's stem that's in the water, shifted to the left and slightly distorted. I draw in the reflection of the stem on the surface of the water. The cat is drawn similarly to the rose in that each part is broken down into basic shapes—modified sphere for the head, cylinders for the body and legs, and a rectangle for the base. Of course I draw it in relation to the surrounding objects. I draw the label on the wine bottle and then I draw a line indicating the back of the table, which helps me check the positioning of my objects. I step back to make sure I have achieved an accurate line drawing as shown here.

Continues

Illustrated Demonstration

Continued

Step 3 | **Block in the Background.**

I block in a value for the background wall and a somewhat lighter one for the table. I try to include as much of the outlines of the objects in the tone of the background. I don't worry about the remaining lines in the interiors of the objects, as they'll be covered in the next step I just want to begin to switch my thinking from line to tone. I smooth the texture of the charcoal strokes with my finger and paper stump. My drawing now looks like this.

Step 4 | **Block in the Tones.**

Since the wine bottle is colored glass, I block in a tone for the local value of that color, being careful to leave the highlights as the white of the paper. There's a colored liquid in this colored glass object, so I fill in a darker tone to represent the combined local value of green glass plus red wine. In the vase, I block in a tone above the water for the value of the background I can see through the glass and a darker tone for the distorted shadow of the background I see in the water. There is a lighter tone underneath that tone and also the shapes of tone for the base of the vase.

For the wine glass, I block in the local value of the wine, leaving white paper for the highlights, and then indicate the reflections on the surface of the wine and on the sides of the glass. The stem of the wine glass is more complicated because the design cut into the stem refracts the light in many directions, creating many different values. I visualize each of these values as a shape and focus on the largest and darkest of these shapes to fill in first. Then I draw the shapes of the middle values and fill in their tone, keeping them flat for now. Then I go back to the bowl of the wine glass and draw in the values I can see through the glass above the wine.

Turning to the rose, I draw in the shadow areas on the stem. I block in tones for the local value of each leaf and another tone for the shadow areas of the flower. Then I block in the shadow areas on the cat. Finally, I block in the cast shadows, leaving me with this tonal study.

Step 5 | **Create Volume.**

As I darken values to create the volume of each object, I constantly squint to compare values throughout the drawing. I begin by darkening obvious shadow areas, knowing that I can lighten the subtle reflections if I need to in the next step. I blend these darker areas into the existing tone, which now represents areas of reflected light, to create the subtle gradations that suggest volume. As I darken the background in order to pull the objects forward in the picture plane, I also darken the background that's seen through clear glass to give the illusion that the viewer is looking through the glass. Many of the dark tones on the wine bottle and the wine in the glass need to be very dark, so I use the compressed charcoal for these areas. There are two labels on the wine bottle, one I see through the glass and one on the outside. I darken the one I see through the glass and gradate the tones on the outside one and the simple graphics. I darken the shadow areas on the leaves and the flower part of the rose. Also, I gradate the tones on the stem to give it more volume. Then I darken and gradate the tones on the cat. I also adjust the values on the tabletop and then the cast shadows. This step is now finished.

Step 6 | **Finish the Drawing.**

Now I'm ready for the subtle finishing touches. Visualizing reflections in the glass objects as shapes in their own right, I adjust the values as I adjust the values around them. I use my kneaded eraser to lighten some when necessary and darken others. I step back frequently to compare my drawing at a distance with the still-life subject, squinting to compare values. If any highlight has gotten some charcoal on it, I remove it with the eraser and reestablish the shape. I narrow my focus to the detail of each object. In order to make the rose my focal point, I want to make as many different values as I can to make as much visual interest as I can. This involves looking at each part of the rose and adjusting all of the values. In some areas I have to adjust the background in order to make more volume in the rose. Remember that the more varied values I can make, the more real my object will appear to be. This will also reinforce this object as the focal point of the drawing. When my lights and darks are balanced to give equal emphasis on both sides of the drawing, and when I can't find any more values to adjust, as shown here, my drawing is finished.

things to remember

- Drawing transparent objects is not difficult as long as you visualize what you see as shapes of different values.

- In a transparent object, unlike a solid one, you can see the object's interior surface, objects placed behind the transparent one, and reflections on the glass object's surface.

- Begin every drawing of a glass object by drawing its basic shape.

- In order to understand what you are seeing through the glass and reflected in the glass, look around at the surrounding objects to identify the shapes you are seeing.

- If the surface of a glass object is curved, what you see through it is distorted, with the distortion being greatest near the edges of the object.

- If a glass object has designs cut into it, this will distort the image of anything you see through the glass.

- Values seen through clear glass should be rendered in the same tones as those of the surrounding objects.

- For colored glass or a colored liquid in a glass object, put a tone over the whole area first to represent the local color, later adding values for any objects seen through the glass or liquid and any reflections.

- Clear liquids such as water can magnify and distort the appearance of anything seen through them.

- The surface of a liquid is usually the light area; it reflects the objects around it.

- Opaque liquids are drawn as if they were solid objects. Most such liquids are at least slightly translucent and therefore transmit a little bit of light.

in review

1. What is the first step in drawing an object made of glass or other transparent material?

2. What is the effect of the curvature of a glass surface on the appearance of objects seen from behind the glass? At what point(s) on the glass surface is this effect greatest?

3. In addition to being able to see the objects behind a glass object, what else can you see in a glass vessel such as a wine glass that you would not be able to see in a glass made of an opaque material such as metal?

4. How is the surface of glass like and unlike the surface of polished metal?

5. What should you do differently when drawing colored glass than when drawing clear glass?

6. What is the effect of a clear liquid such as water on objects seen through it?

7. How is a nearly opaque liquid such as milk different from a clear liquid such as water?

project

Choose three or four glass objects for this charcoal drawing, with perhaps one additional non-transparent object such as the rose in this chapter's illustrated demonstration. If possible, choose at least one colored glass object, and put liquid in at least one of the glass objects. Better yet, put two different liquids—water and a colored liquid such as wine or juice—in two of the objects. Pick a cloth that has a middle to dark value for the background, so that you will clearly see its value through the glass. Choose one object to be the focal point and place it in the foreground near the center, arranging the other objects around and behind it in a balanced and unified composition. Place your photoflood lamp so that it shines strongly on the focal point. Remember to draw the shapes of the glass objects before you turn your attention to the values you can see through the glass or as reflections.

homework

Choose four glass objects you would like to draw. Try a variety of clear glass and colored glass, keeping in mind that faceted glass makes the objects you see through it more complex to draw. Put water in one clear glass object, and maybe something in the water, such as a straw. Put a colored liquid in another glass object. As you draw the objects, remember to fill in the tones that you can see through the glass so that the objects look transparent. Complete four pencil drawings on 11 × 14 cold-press paper.

Additional Media

Objectives:

Describe the difference between dry and wet drawing media.

Experiment with new drawing media: charcoal on toned paper, Conté crayon, pen and ink, and brush and ink.

Describe the materials needed for drawing with these media.

Introduction

Now that you've learned the techniques of accurate still-life drawing using charcoal and graphite pencils, you may be ready to try some new media. This chapter introduces you to new dry and wet media, including charcoal on toned paper, Conté crayon, and ink with either a pen or a brush.

BEYOND CHARCOAL AND PENCIL

So far in this book you've worked with only two media, charcoal and graphite pencil. Sticking to these two similar media has allowed you to concentrate on learning to draw without being overwhelmed by a variety of media. Every drawing medium has its own nuances, and it takes time and practice to get used to working with each one. Now that you've honed your drawing skills by using two of the most forgiving and flexible media available, you may be ready to branch out and try something new. This chapter introduces you to several new drawing tools and tells you which kinds of paper work best with each. Try them all! Experiment to find which media work best for you. Every artist is different, and you may find that your drawing skills are better suited to some medium other than charcoal or pencil. Working with a new medium takes practice. In order to get to know the peculiarities of a new medium, play around with it before you try to do a finished drawing.

Drawing media fall into two categories: dry and wet. **Dry media** go on to the paper dry. Charcoal and pencil are dry media. This chapter will introduce you to two additional dry media: white charcoal and Conté crayon. **Wet media** go on wet, in a liquid or semiliquid form, and then dry on the paper as the liquid in which the pigment is suspended evaporates. With wet media, you can either draw with the full-strength pigment or dilute it if it's water-soluble, which gives you the ability to make a variety of different tones with the same medium.

All of these drawing media are available in any art supply store. Different media require different papers; for instance, the newsprint you've been using for charcoal drawings will not hold up to wet media. If in doubt, ask the salesperson what kind of paper to use with a given medium. Some stores will allow you to experiment with the drawing tools and scraps of paper to see what suits you best, or you may want to buy sheets of several different kinds of paper so you can experiment at home.

DRY MEDIA

You're familiar with the basics of using dry media from your study of charcoal and pencil drawing. Now it's time to add another dimension to your drawing with black and white charcoal on toned paper and with Conté crayon.

Black and White Charcoal on Toned Paper

When you draw in charcoal on white paper, the paper itself represents the lightest value in your gray scale, value 1. However, charcoal or pastel paper is available in a wide variety of tones, from light grays through black, as well as in colors. When you draw on **toned paper,** the value of the paper is no longer value 1. For instance, the drawing in Figure 12-1 was done on a toned paper of value 4. Anything that is a value 4 in the drawing has been left as the tone of the paper. Vine charcoal was, as usual, used to build up the values that are darker than value 4. For values 1, 2, and 3 white charcoal was added to lighten the value of the paper and extend the gray scale. The pure of the charcoal, rather than the white of the paper, thus represents the highlights of your drawing.

Drawing with white charcoal means that you have to reverse your thinking about tone. When working with vine charcoal, you add more charcoal to darken a given area. When working with white charcoal, however, adding more charcoal has the effect of *lightening* an area. If you use only a little white charcoal, the value of the paper will show

Figure | **12-1** |

through, and that area will be darker than one that you cover more completely. When you start working with white charcoal, choose a paper that is relatively light in value, like the value 4 paper used in Figure 12-1. When you get used to drawing in reverse, you can try a darker value paper. Eventually you may want to try drawing on black paper. Then you would use no black charcoal, only white, and the entire drawing would be done in reverse; you'd be building up lights rather than darks. It takes some practice to switch your thinking in this way.

Charcoal paper has a rougher surface texture than does newsprint. The surface texture of the paper is called **tooth.** The more tooth, the rougher the texture. Newsprint has very little tooth, while toned charcoal papers have more. On a paper with more tooth, the charcoal sits only on the raised surface of the paper, so that the drawing has a grainy appearance. The more tooth the paper has, the grainier the appearance of the drawing. Some charcoal papers are smoother, or have less tooth, on one side than on the other. You can use whichever side you choose; test your charcoal on a small area of both sides to see which texture you prefer.

The process of drawing on toned paper is basically the same as that for drawing on white paper. Start with the vine charcoal and lightly sketch in the basic shapes and modifications as usual. Be aware that it's more difficult to erase from charcoal paper than from newsprint because of the tooth of the paper. Block in your background and shadow areas as usual, ignoring the light areas for the moment. Build up the dark tones with your vine charcoal to create as much volume as you can, remembering to leave the areas that are the same value as the paper untouched.

Then pick up your white charcoal and start working in reverse, beginning with a light application of white charcoal to represent the areas that are only a little lighter in value than the paper.

Continue building up the light tones until you reach pure white for the highlights. Don't use white charcoal for reflected light. For one thing, reflected light is never as light as the highlight. For another, mixing white charcoal with black can make your drawing look muddy. If you need to lighten an area that already has vine charcoal on it, use a kneader eraser, chamois, or finger to remove vine charcoal rather than adding white charcoal. Also, if you need to use a paper stump or a finger to blend the white charcoal, make sure you use a clean one so you won't get any surprise gray streaks.

Conté Crayon

Conté crayon is a well-known French chalk in which pigments are mixed with clay and water, pressed into sticks, and baked in a kiln. You can also get Conté pencils. Conté comes in black, white, and two colors: *sanguine,* which is red, and *bistre,* which is a sepia or dark brown color. Use only one of the colors to work with when you first start out getting used to the medium. The drawing in Figure 12-2 is done in black Conté on white paper.

A drawing done in Conté crayon is similar in appearance to a charcoal drawing. You can get smooth lines and rich, dark tones with Conté, but it is more difficult both to blend and to erase than is charcoal. You can use almost any kind of paper with Conté crayon; as with charcoal, a paper with more tooth gives a grainier appearance to the drawing. If you choose a toned paper, use white Conté for the light areas and highlights.

Because Conté crayon is difficult to erase, begin your drawing with light pencil lines, sketching in

Figure | 12-2 | the basic shapes and modifying them to look like the objects you're seeing. Then block in the background and shadow areas as usual with the Conté, working lightly to gradually build up gradated tones. The more Conté you put down, the darker the tone—unless, of course, you're working in white Conté, which has the opposite effect. You want to avoid going too dark too soon, because it's so difficult to lighten Conté once you've put it down. If you do need to lighten an area, don't use white Conté! As with charcoal, mixing the chalks will give your drawing a muddy appearance. Instead, try using your kneaded eraser. If you need to go a lot lighter, you might need a Pink Pearl eraser, which you can get at the art supply store. If you're using toned paper, leave areas that are the same value as the paper untouched.

Figure |12-3|

Another technique for getting soft, gradated tones similar to the look of charcoal is to make a dry wash of Conté crayon. To do so, you'll need to buy a sand block like the one shown in Figure 12-3. This inexpensive item is very versatile; besides using it to make your dry wash you can also sharpen charcoal and graphite pencils on it. To make a dry wash, simply rub the crayon across the surface of the sandpaper to loosen the pigment. Dip a clean paper stump or a wad of tissue into the pigment dust and apply the pigment to the paper, one layer at a time. Using a paper stump allows you to actually draw with this loose pigment. If you run out of loose pigment, it's easy to make more.

Experiment with both methods, drawing with the crayons and using dry wash, before attempting a finished drawing. Try several different papers with varying amounts of tooth to see whether you prefer a drawing with more or less grain.

WET MEDIA

The main wet medium for drawing is ink. There are a wide variety of kinds of ink, in many different colors; the choice depends on the kind of pen or brush you want to draw with. The most popular ink for drawing is **India ink,** which comes in two varieties: waterproof and water-soluble. **Waterproof ink** has had shellac added to it so that it becomes permanent when it dries. This feature is important if you plan to combine an ink line drawing with washes or some other wet media. The advantage of **water-soluble ink** is that it will not clog your pen or brush when it dries.

You can use either pens or brushes for drawing in ink. Whatever instrument you choose, always end your session by rinsing the pen or brush with water to remove the ink. Removing the ink will help keep your drawing instrument in good shape; this is particularly important when you're using waterproof ink.

Pen and Ink

A pen-and-ink drawing has a very different look from a charcoal drawing. Drawing with a pen is entirely linear. Rather than blocking in subtle gradated tones to represent different values, you draw lines. You can draw in outline or contour, and then fill in tones with a variety of lines. You can draw in a loose, sketchy way, or you can go for a more controlled look with a fuller rendering of tones, depending on what line technique you use. The beauty of working in pen and ink is that it's perfect for quick sketches, as when you're drawing on location. The biggest drawback is that you can't erase any mistakes you make—but then, mistakes can add to the spontaneity of a drawing.

Materials

A variety of **pen points and nibs** are available to give you a range of different kinds of lines in ink drawing. A drawing nib is flexible and gives you a variety of line widths depending on how you hold it. Such nibs come in many shapes and sizes. Another useful point or nib is a crow quill pen, which is good for drawing details because it gives a very fine line. You also need holders for your points and nibs; nibs have one kind of pen holder and crow quill points use a smaller holder. Both kinds of holders, nibs and points are relatively inexpensive. Ask the salesperson at the art supply store to show you a few different pens. You can use these pens with India ink or another ink if you prefer. To draw, you dip the pen point into the ink, draw until the pen runs out of ink, and dip again. When you finish, wash the pen under running water, removing the nib or point for storage so that it doesn't rust inside the penholder, and dry both nib and holder thoroughly.

A **technical pen** is less flexible because it creates a line width that is always consistent. For a different line width, you have to buy a different size point, though you can put different points into the same penholder. The points are more expensive than drawing nibs or crow quill points. However, a technical pen can be useful if you want to sketch on location, where having an open bottle of ink would be inconvenient, because technical pens carry their own ink supply. You can't use India ink in a technical pen; there's a special kind of ink designed for technical pens that prevents clogging. Cleaning a technical pen is difficult, so it's important to replace the cap on the pen to keep the ink from drying in the point and clogging it up. If ink does dry in the point, try moistening the tip with water to remove the dry ink, and then gently shake the pen to get the ink flowing again. If you don't use the pen for a long time, the ink might dry inside the cartridge as well, and then you'll have to clean it. Taking the pen point apart is difficult, especially for the smaller points, and is likely to damage the delicate workings. You're better off investing in an ultrasonic cleaner.

The paper for pen-and-ink drawing should be a smooth surface with little or no tooth. A rough surface will catch the point of the pen, giving you uneven lines. A fine crow quill point will catch in almost any surface texture and create a blob or splatter. Furthermore, the texture of paper with tooth acts like a blotter; the ink spreads to give you a heavier line than you intended. So what you want is something called **hot-press paper,** which is very smooth with virtually no tooth. If you're using a technical pen, you want something even smoother, a paper with what is called a **plate finish.** Try experimenting with several different kinds of smooth paper to see what works best with the pen you're using.

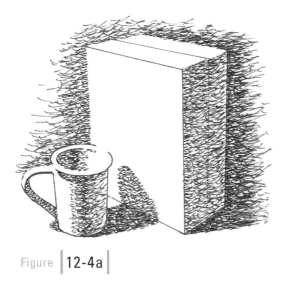

Figure | 12-4a |

Figure | 12-4b |

Techniques

Creating volume using pen and ink is quite different from work-ing in charcoal. Instead of blocking in tones, you build up various kinds of lines to create different values. Figure 12-4 shows the same subject matter rendered in different ways using different kinds of lines to build up the tones. Varying the line technique changes the value of the tones.

One way to vary the tones in your ink drawing is to vary the thick-ness of the line, which you can do easily with a drawing nib or point by changing the angle at which you hold the pen and the amount of pressure you apply. You can also vary the distance between lines to

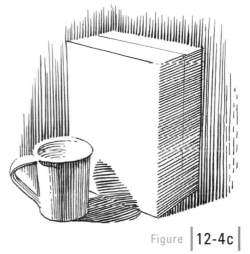

Figure | 12-4c |

create lighter or darker tones, as shown in Figure 12-5. Another method is **crosshatching,** which involves combining horizontal, vertical, and diagonal lines, as demonstrated in Figure 12-6. The more lines you crisscross, the darker the value will become.

Because you're working with lines, you won't be able render a full range of values as you do with charcoal. The value scale for a pen-and-ink drawing has only about seven steps, rather than the ten for charcoal. As you can see in Figure 12-7, the extremes of the scale are the same as for charcoal—the white of the paper and a solid black—but you can render only about five tones between these two extremes. You still need to render the shadow areas in order to define the volume of your objects, so where you will eliminate the subtle gradations of tone you're used to drawing in charcoal will be in the light areas. Squint to eliminate the subtle tone vari-ations in the light areas, and leave the light areas the white of the paper without rendering the highlights. Especially when you're first starting out, make sure you have a good strong light on your subject so that you'll clearly see the separation between light and dark areas and be able to draw the shadow patterns that define the forms of the objects.

The best way to get comfortable with working in line rather than in tone is to practice on simple subject matter. Go back to the basic shapes. You might start with some of the projects in Chapters 3–7, or set up a simple still life with only two or three objects of the same basic shape. Make sure you have strong light on your objects, and then do several quick pen-and-ink drawings of the same subject, trying a different line technique

Figure | 12-6 |

Figure | 12-5 |

Figure | 12-7 |

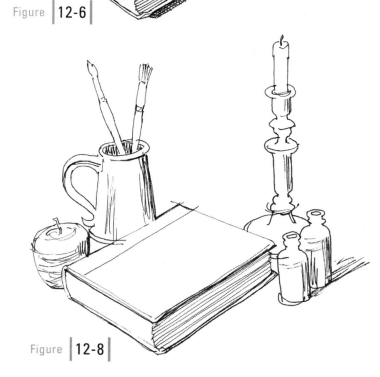

Figure | 12-8 |

for each one. After you become familiar with a few line techniques that feel comfortable to you, you'll be ready to tackle a finished drawing.

The big advantage of pen-and-ink sketching is its spontaneous feel. However, nothing kills the feeling of spontaneity more quickly than fear of making a mistake in a medium that can't be erased. So if you want to do a finished drawing, you might start by drawing the basic shapes and modifying them in pencil. Once you've got an accurate line drawing, switch to the pen and draw over the pencil lines and then fill in the tones with line. Any stray pencil marks can be erased when you're finished. Overworking your drawing will kill the spontaneous feel.

One of the nice things about pen and ink is it is great for quick sketches. Draw loosely to capture a quick impression of what you see, as in Figure 12-8. Let your mistakes live in your drawing—they add to the spontaneous feel and give charm to your drawing.

Brush and Ink

Another way to draw in ink is by using a brush. A brush gives an entirely different look than does a pen; it gives much more fluid lines. You can also dilute the ink with water and use it either to draw lines or to paint washes that, when dry, create soft, gradated tones. The more you dilute the ink, the lighter the tone you will create. Figure 12-9 is an example of an ink-wash drawing. The look is similar to that of a monochromatic (one-color) watercolor painting. Once you learn how to control lines and washes with a brush, you may like the flexibility of drawing in ink and the way the ink and brush respond.

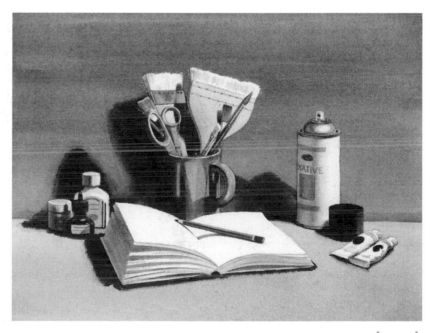

Figure |**12-9**|

Materials

To do brush-and-ink drawings, obviously you need not only India or similar ink but also at least one brush. You need a round brush in the family called **watercolor brushes,** like the one shown in Figure 12-10. Such brushes come in a variety of sizes, using either natural or synthetic bristles. Synthetic bristles are usually less expensive. The size of the brush is indicated by a number; the higher the number, the larger the brush. The size in which you want to draw will determine the size of brush you should buy. You might want to start with a large brush for drawing major lines and doing large washes of tone plus a smaller brush for detail work.

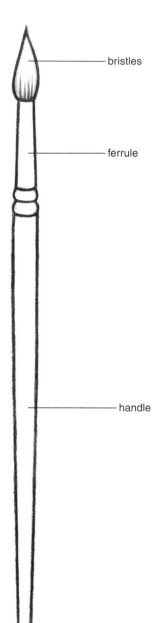

bristles

ferrule

handle

Figure | 12-10 |

Watercolor brushes have short handles and are designed to be held as you hold a pencil. Note how the bristles of the brush in Figure 12-10 are fat near the ferrule, which joins them to the handle, and taper to a point at the end. If you hold the brush at an angle or press down on it lightly, you'll get a fat line; hold it straight with almost no pressure and you'll get a very fine line—and you can do both in the same brushstroke! That's part of what makes ink-brush drawings look so fluid.

It's important to clean your brushes thoroughly after every drawing session. First rinse out the excess pigment under running water. Then use a small amount of mild soap to clean the brush thoroughly and rinse again. Finally, squeeze or shake out the excess water and shape the bristles into a point with your fingers. Store the brush upright or lying on a surface that doesn't allow it to roll in order to protect the bristles.

You also need a different kind of paper to work in this wet medium, especially if you're going to use washes. **Watercolor paper** is designed to take a lot of water without disintegrating. You have a wide variety of kinds of watercolor paper to choose from. If you're going to work wet-on-wet, as described next, you want a thick paper; if you'll be using few washes and a relatively dry brush, you can get away with a thinner paper. Various textures are available, from hot-press paper with hardly any tooth through cold-press paper to rough paper. The choice is up to you, depending on how much texture you want to see in your drawing. You may want to try several different kinds of paper.

Watercolor paper can be expensive. You can buy it in single sheets, in a pad, or in a block. Blocks are great if you want to work really wet, because each sheet of paper is tacked down to the pad all the way around the edges, so that it buckles hardly at all, no matter how much water you put on it, and dries flat. After the ink dries, you can cut the sheet of paper away from the block with a utility knife or razor blade.

Techniques

You'll definitely want to practice with your brush and ink before you start a finished drawing; there are a wide variety of ways of working with a brush that give a whole range of different effects, such as those shown in Figure 12-11. Besides drawing on dry paper with full-strength ink, you can dilute the ink with water to create different lines and tones. One interesting technique that's not possible with dry media is working wet on wet: You moisten the paper before you even begin to draw on it. Even if you use a brush fully loaded with full-strength ink, this technique gives you softer lines and tones than working on dry paper. Another variation is to dilute the ink itself with water and then apply it with the brush to either wet or dry paper.

These techniques give you a wide variety of tones and effects, but you do have to know how to control them. Even after you've practiced, you'll find that occasionally something happens that you weren't expecting. Such "happy accidents" are part of the joy of working in a wet medium. When they happen, leave them alone. They give a fresh, spontaneous feel to your drawing.

MORE EXPERIMENTS

You don't have to stop with the media discussed in this chapter. You can draw with anything that makes a mark: ballpoint pens, fountain pens, watercolor pencils, felt-tip markers, and various kinds of brushes. Go to the art supply store and look at the various possibilities for drawing. Try different kinds of paper as well, smoother or rougher, thicker or thinner. There's no law that says you can't use paper designed for a wet medium with dry media. You may want to combine media as well. Some media work better together than others, but experiment to find which ones work well for you. Just make sure you practice before you attempt a finished drawing. Beyond that, be adventurous and have fun!

SUMMARY

The most important thing to remember when you try a new medium is to experiment and play with your medium before you attempt a finished drawing. Each medium has its own characteristics and nuances, so it takes practice to get used to each one. Each of the media discussed in this chapter—black and white charcoal on toned paper, Conté crayon, or ink with either a pen or a brush—is suitable for still-life drawing. In the next chapter, you'll begin to explore two other important kinds of drawing: figure drawing and landscape drawing.

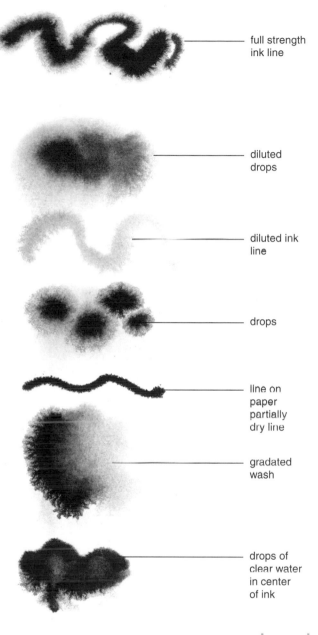

full strength ink line

diluted drops

diluted ink line

drops

line on paper partially dry line

gradated wash

drops of clear water in center of ink

Figure | **12-11** |

things to remember

- Dry media are those that stay dry throughout the drawing process. Black and white charcoals, pencils, and Conté crayons are dry media.

- Wet media are applied wet and then they dry on the paper. Ink is a wet medium.

- Working in charcoal on toned paper requires a switch in thinking about tone in that the tone of the paper represents a darker value rather than value 1 in the drawing. Values lighter than that of the paper are achieved with the application of white charcoal.

- Conté crayon, which comes in two colors as well as black and white, is similar to charcoal but gives a different look.

- Conté is difficult to erase and to blend in order to achieve soft gradations of tone.

- Drawing in pen and ink requires switching your thinking from tone to line, because values in the shadow areas of a drawing are made with a combination of lines.

- Working in ink with a brush rather than a pen allows you to achieve fluid lines and soft gradations of tone.

- Each medium requires its own tools and paper.

- Each medium requires new techniques. It's important to experiment with any new medium to learn its peculiarities before attempting a finished drawing.

in review

1. What is the difference between a dry medium and a wet medium?

2. Name two dry media and one wet medium.

3. Define "tooth" in reference to drawing papers.

4. What is a good technique for beginning a drawing in a medium that is difficult or impossible to erase such as Conté crayon or ink?

5. What is the main difference between drawing in charcoal on toned paper and on white paper?

6. Name two differences between Conté crayon and charcoal.

7. What is the name of the kind of smooth-textured paper that is best for pen-and-ink drawing?

8. What kind of paper is best for a drawing in which you intend to use ink washes?

project

Choose one of the media discussed in this chapter. Experiment with it by drawing some quick sketches, seeing how many different ways you can shade to suggest the form of an object. When you feel comfortable with your new medium, set up a simple still life: either go back to one of the still-life set-ups you did in the projects of Chapters 3–7 or choose new objects to draw—just make sure that all of them are simple rather than complex shapes. Be sure to place a strong, direct light on your subject to reveal the forms you need to draw. Practice, with your new medium, the techniques you've learned in this book for accurately rendering the shape and form of objects.

homework

Choose another new medium and experiment with it. Choose four objects with the same basic shape and make drawings of each one individually, using your new medium.

Beyond Still Life

3

Objectives:

Understand the basic shapes that underlie the human figure.

Describe the proportions of the ideal or average human figure.

Understand foreshortening and describe its effects on the appearance of the figure.

Learn to draw the human figure using the same techniques as for still-life drawing.

Know how to frame a landscape drawing in order to choose the subject to be drawn.

Learn to sketch the basic shapes of a landscape drawing and then work quickly to fill in volume before the light changes.

Create the illusion of space in landscape drawing.

Render a variety of textures in natural objects.

Introduction

Now that you're thoroughly familiar with still-life drawing and have explored some additional media beyond charcoal and pencil, you may be interested in learning about how to draw other subjects. This chapter introduces you to the two other most important kinds of drawings: figure drawings and landscape drawings.

BEYOND STILL LIFE

EXPANDING YOUR DRAWING HORIZONS

The process you have learned for drawing still lifes can be applied to anything you want to draw. If you can simplify an object into basic shapes, modify it to look like what you're seeing, and give it volume with shading, you can draw a human head or a complete figure, a tree or a whole landscape. Sighting techniques remain crucial to get proportions and angles right, just as in still-life drawing. Human figures and landscapes are somewhat more complicated than still lifes, and you can take courses in either one. This chapter will introduce you to some of the basics of figure and landscape drawing, showing you how to apply the techniques you've already learned to these new subjects.

FIGURE DRAWING

Centuries of artistic experience have shown that the best way to learn to draw the human figure is to draw a nude model from life. Clothing complicates the figure; you need to understand the underlying form beneath the clothing in order to render both the figure and the fabric that covers it. So look for an opportunity to have a nude model pose for you. Many art schools and associations have sketch classes you can join for a nominal fee. If this isn't possible, you're still better off learning to draw nudes than getting people to pose for you in their clothing, so instead copy from other artists' works or draw from photographs. Your local library has books of works by the "old masters"; if you're lucky, you may even find a book of photographs of nude models.

The Whole Figure

When you start a figure drawing, you visualize the entire figure (and whatever background you choose to include in your drawing) as one shape, just as in still-life drawing, and position that single shape on the page. Marking the position and shape of the figure as a whole on the page will prevent a common problem beginning art students often have: They start drawing the head and work their way down the body to find they don't have room on the page for the feet! Even if you measure a figure out as eight heads, as explained next, if you don't scale the image down to fit the paper, you may run out of paper before you run out of figure.

Though the human figure is more complicated than the average still-life subject, the process is still the same. It's vitally important to get the shapes, angles, and proportions right—to achieve an accurate line drawing—before you begin filling in volume. As in any complex object, drawing one part incorrectly will throw the whole rest of the drawing off. Use your sighting techniques and horizontal and vertical plumb lines to ensure that you have drawn each body part accurately in relation to the rest of the figure. Use the negative space to double-check the positions of each part. Step back from your drawing to compare it to your subject, and make sure it looks like the outline of what you are seeing before you start filling in the volume. It's much easier to erase at this stage than it will be after you've added the shading.

The Basic Shapes in the Human Figure

The human figure as a whole is a complex object. Like any complex object, it can be broken down into a set of basic shapes. The simplified form in Figure 13-1 shows the basic shapes of the human body; it's mostly a collection of cylindrical shapes except for the heads, hands, and feet. The torsos of male and female forms are somewhat different. In Figure 13-2, the male torso consists of two cylinders separated at the waist; the lower torso is a modified cylinder. The male genitalia can be broken down into a modified cylinder and two modified spheres. However, in the female form on the right, the upper and lower torso are modified cones. The female figure's upper torso tapers inward toward the waist and the lower torso tapers outward toward the hips. The breasts, near the top of the torso, are modified spheres. Otherwise, the male and female forms are about the same. The arms are two cylinders, separated at the elbow; the legs, likewise, are cylinders separated at the knee. The neck is a cylinder; the head is egg-shaped—a modified sphere. The hands and feet themselves are complex forms consisting of a rectangular shape together with cylinders for the fingers and toes. When you draw hands and feet, you'll treat the fingers and toes as one shape at first and later break them into individual forms.

All of this refers to the basic human form, but of course, every human being is different. In figure drawing, once you've seen and sketched the basic shapes, you modify the form to make it look like what you're seeing. Knowledge of human anatomy is invaluable in this process. Just as understanding the basic shapes helps you simplify and draw an object, so understanding the structure of bones and muscles that underlies the human form can help you modify the basic shapes into human body parts. Knowing how the bones are connected and where the muscles and ligaments lie, and what happens to these underlying structures when the body moves, helps you understand what you're seeing on the surface of the human form you're trying to draw. There are books on human anatomy specifically for artists; get one and study it, and keep it nearby whenever you're doing a figure drawing. You'll need lots of practice in drawing the human form from many angles in many different poses before you really master figure drawing, but your knowledge of basic shapes and of the underlying anatomy will start the simplification process in your brain that makes the drawing easier to do.

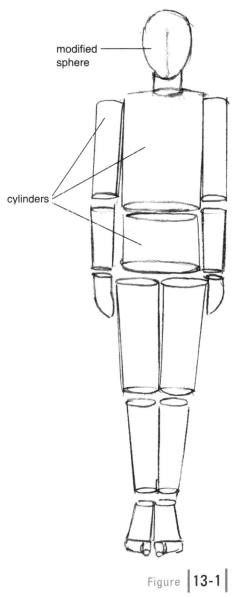

modified sphere

cylinders

Figure |**13-1**|

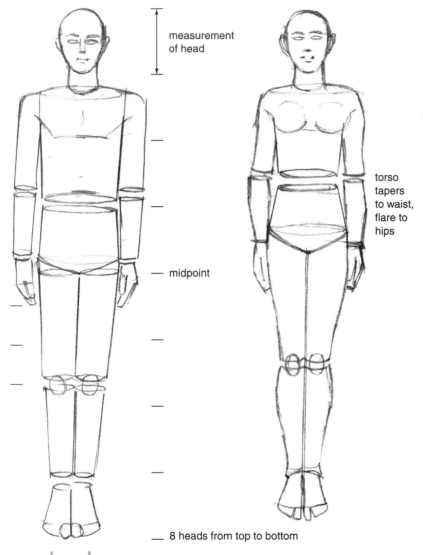

measurement of head

torso tapers to waist, flare to hips

— midpoint

_ 8 heads from top to bottom

Figure | 13-2 |

Human Proportion

Though human beings all differ slightly in their proportions, knowing the basic proportions of the ideal human figure can help you block in your figure at the outset, before you modify it to match the actual person you're drawing. Your sighting skills will help you establish the proper proportions. The average human adult, when standing, is approximately eight heads high, as you can see from Figure 13-2. If you measure the height of the head you're drawing with your charcoal, you can then mark eight of those measurements to give you the height of the ideal adult figure. (The head of a child is larger in proportion to the body; how much larger depends on the age of the child.) Here's another ideal measurement that can help you avoid a common problem: the midpoint of the ideal adult when standing is the crotch. Measure from the top of the head to the crotch, mark that midpoint on your paper, and then double that measurement to give you the position of the feet. If you use this measurement, you'll never end up with the upper body drawn in correct proportion while the legs are too short.

Continuing with the ideal adult figure, the upper torso is approximately two heads high and the pelvis is one head high. Note, too, the length of the arms: The tips of the fingers reach about a third of the way down the thigh. The elbow falls just about at the waist. Another common problem beginning students have is making the feet too short. Surprisingly enough, the foot is as long as the forearm from wrist to elbow. Of course, the position of the foot on the floor will affect how you perceive its length, as you'll see in the next section. And remember, these are ideal proportions. Your model will not be ideal. Use these average proportions as beginning guidelines and then sight and measure to accurately capture the proportions of the actual figure you are drawing.

Foreshortening

You've already learned that objects that are closer to you appear larger than those that are farther away. This phenomenon, called *perspective* when it's applied to an object, is called **foreshortening** when applied to a human figure. The angle at which you view the figure, as in still-life drawing, affects the way in which you perceive the spatial depth of a given body part. For instance, in Figure 13-3, the left forearm of the model is foreshortened because it is coming forward in the picture plane. That arm appears much shorter than does the right arm just like a cylinder on its side. You know that both arms are approximately the same size, but you have to draw what you see, not what you think you should be seeing. The same principle applies to legs or feet—if one foot is closer to you than the other, it will appear larger.

The more extreme the angle at which you view the figure, the more pronounced the foreshortening will be. In Figure 13-4, the entire body is foreshortened; the head, which is closest to you, appears larger than the rest of the figure. This figure certainly isn't eight heads high! The ideal body proportions don't apply when you're drawing a foreshortened figure. Always take note of your eye level in relation to your model so that you will be able to capture the perspective of the basic shapes correctly. Then you'll be able to draw the proportions of the body parts exactly as you see them so that your drawing will look realistic.

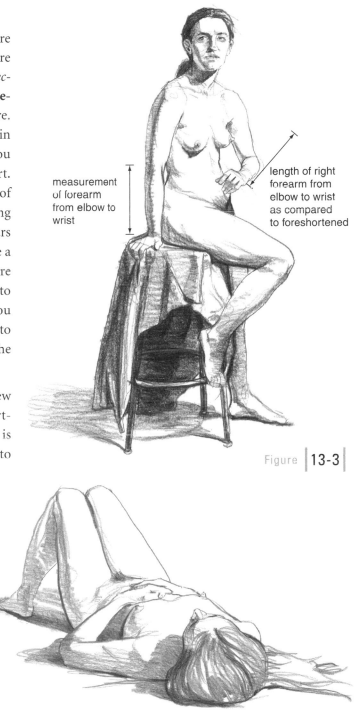

measurement of forearm from elbow to wrist

length of right forearm from elbow to wrist as compared to foreshortened

Figure | 13-3 |

Figure | 13-4 |

The Gesture

Perhaps the most important difference between a still-life subject and a human model is that the human model is alive. Though the figure you're drawing isn't moving at the moment, there is energy or movement in the pose. This energy is called the **gesture** of the pose.

imaginary line that
captures the gesture of
the pose

Figure | 13-5 |

If you accurately render each body part but don't capture the gesture, you haven't yet done a realistic drawing. Even lying down or sitting still takes energy; when the model takes an active pose, as in Figure 13-5, the gesture is even more pronounced. Imagine the energy of the gesture as a thread or line that runs through the center of the body beginning at the top of the head, down through the neck along the spine to the supporting leg or the leg closest to you. Another way to capture the gesture is to feel the energy in your own body. Imagine yourself in the same pose as the model, and see how your body feels and where the energy runs. Keep this energy in mind as you are drawing. Capturing the gesture is vital to making your figures look alive.

Creating Volume

Once you have made an accurate line drawing of your figure, with all the proportions and relationships correct, you're ready to start giving the figure volume. As in still-life drawing, rendering the volume is much easier if you have a strong direct light on the subject.

If you have the luxury of a long pose, you can begin by blocking in the background values as you do in a still-life drawing, covering up the outlines of the figure as you go. If the pose is shorter, concentrate on the values in the shadow areas of the figure itself and, for now, leave some of the lines that represent the edges. The lines will remain visible in the light areas, but you'll be able to cover the lines in the shadow areas as you block in the values of the shadows. Be sure to note the direction of the light source, and then begin blocking in the largest shadow areas. Use your understanding of the volume of the basic shapes to help you. Since most of the figure's underlying basic shapes are cylinders, the volume of the shapes you're seeing is round. Work over the entire figure, blocking in the shadow patterns as shapes in their own right. At this stage, you should have a sense of the volume of the subject even though your drawing is still rough.

To complete the drawing, follow the same steps as for a still-life drawing. Continue working over the entire figure to darken some shadow areas and create more volume. Remember that greater contrast in values brings an area forward in the picture plane. You use this principle not only to make an arm or a thigh appear round, but also to show which parts of the body are closer to the viewer than other parts. In Figure 13-6, the model's buttocks are

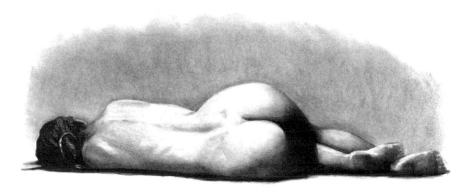

Figure | 13-6 |

not only round but also closest to the viewer, so the contrast in values is great there. You see less contrast of values on the legs and feet, which are farther from the viewer. As in any subject, you'll see reflected light in the shadow areas, though this light is never as light in value as the areas that are being illuminated directly by the light source. Squint constantly to compare values.

If the model is lean, you're likely to be able to see muscles under the skin. These muscles may create their own shadow patterns. Knowledge of anatomy will help you understand and simplify what you're seeing, so keep your artist's anatomy book handy. Knowing what those muscles actually look like under the skin will help you make sense of the shadow patterns. Then squint to see the shapes and copy them exactly as you see them.

Hands and Feet

Many students avoid drawing the hands and feet of a human figure because these extremities seem so complicated. While it's true that hands and feet are more complicated than, say, a leg, they can still be broken down into basic shapes, and seeing these basic shapes enables you to simplify and then draw what you are seeing. It's a good idea to practice drawing these more complicated forms separately from a complete figure. Luckily, you can be your own model for this practice! The hand you don't use for drawing and your bare feet can be your models. Draw them from many different angles in many different poses; hold objects of different shapes in your hand. Once you've had this practice, you'll find it easier to draw the hands and feet of a complete figure.

Start by visualizing the basic shapes. As you can see from Figure 13-7, the palm of the hand is a rectangular, or modified cubic, shape. The fingers are cylindrical. As you begin, draw the palm first and then the fingers as a group. Don't worry about rendering the individual fingers at first, but do draw the thumb as a separate shape. Break the fingers as a group into sections from the first arc of the knuckles at the palm to the second arc of the next knuckles. Then draw them from the second arc to the last knuckle if the fingers are bent in this way; otherwise you can draw from the second arc directly to the tips of the fingers. Figure 13-8 shows how to draw

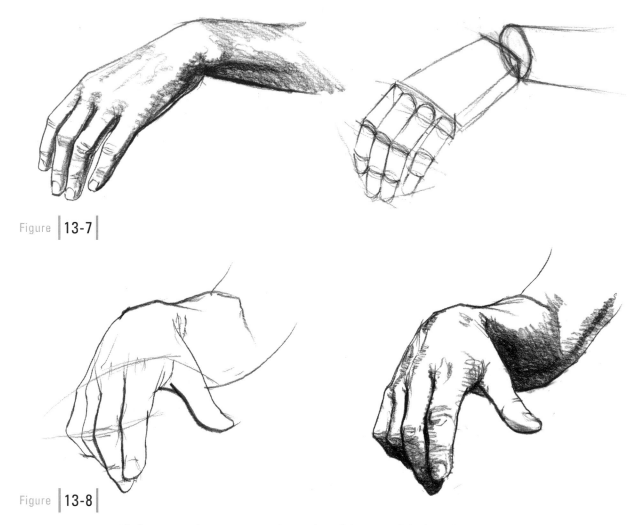

Figure | 13-7 |

Figure | 13-8 |

guide lines in order to capture the angles of the arcs of the knuckles. Accurately rendering these arcs captures the gesture that gives energy to your drawing. Once you have drawn the angles of the knuckles, you can begin to render the individual fingers, using the negative space to help you capture the relationships among them. Then, as usual, you modify the basic shapes to match what you're seeing and then shade your drawing to give it volume.

Similarly, the foot can be broken into basic shapes. From the front, as shown in Figure 13-9, the foot is a rectangular shape and the toes are cylindrical. From the side, the foot is a modified rectangle that is more triangular in shape, but the toes remain cylindrical. Foreshortening is often very important in drawing a foot; when the subject is standing, depending on your eye level, the foreshortening can be extreme, with the toes appearing much larger than the back of the foot. As with the hand, draw the large shape of the foot first and then the toes as a group, including the big toe. Toes are not as articulated as fingers, so it's easy to draw them as a group; as with the fingers, you must capture the arc of the toe knuckles by drawing a guide line. After you've gotten the toes as a group, you can draw them individually and modify the basic shapes to look like the real foot you're drawing.

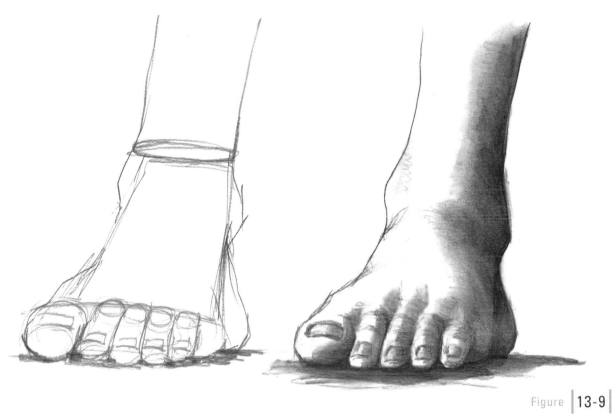

Figure | 13-9 |

The Head

The head is the most complex body part to draw. Capturing a true likeness of a person requires an understanding of the subtle nuances of the head and various facial parts, as well as how they relate to each other; it's a form of precision drawing. When you're starting out, keep it simple: Get the basics drawn and don't worry about capturing a likeness. A lot of practice in drawing only heads and faces will enable you to capture a likeness. It's easy to get this practice because there are people everywhere! Carry a small sketchpad and pencil wherever you go so you can draw quick sketches of heads and faces. Get friends and family to pose for you for longer drawing sessions. Over time you will start to recognize the subtleties of heads and facial features by drawing them from many different angles.

Basic Shapes and Proportions

The basic shape of the human head is a sphere modified into an egg shape. As you can see in Figure 13-10, when the head is seen from the front, the egg is upright; when seen from the side, the head's egg shape is tilted at a 45-degree angle. This egg shape sits atop the cylindrical shape of the neck.

It's useful to know the ideal proportions of the human head, shown in Figure 13-11 with guide lines marked to represent the positions of the facial features. The eyes are located halfway between the top of the head and the bottom of the chin. The bottom of the nose is halfway

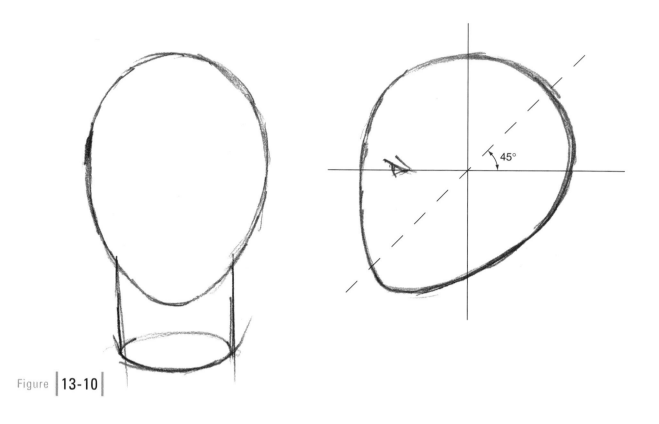

Figure | 13-10 |

between the eyes and the bottom of the chin. Divide the space in half again to find that the bottom of the lip is halfway between the bottom of the nose and the chin. The ears fall between the eyes and the bottom of the nose; exactly where they fall depends on the size of the ears. These proportions are the same no matter whether you are seeing the head straight on, in profile, or in three-quarter view.

From the front, the nose is seen in the center of the egg shape, with its corners of the nostrils lining up vertically with the inside corners of the eyes. The corners of the mouth line up directly under the pupils of the eyes. There is one eye width between the two eyes, and one more eye width from the eye to the side of the head. In other words, the head is five eye widths wide at its widest point.

Of course, if every head corresponded to these ideal proportions, everyone would look alike! It's good to use these ideal proportions when you're first starting out, but when you're ready to start capturing likenesses, you'll have to precisely measure exactly what each feature looks like and where it is placed in relation to the other features.

Perspective

Drawing the head also requires your understanding of elliptical and linear perspective. Imagine strings running through the eyes, across the bottom of the nose, and along the mouth. If you see the head from eye level, these strings form straight lines. However, be-

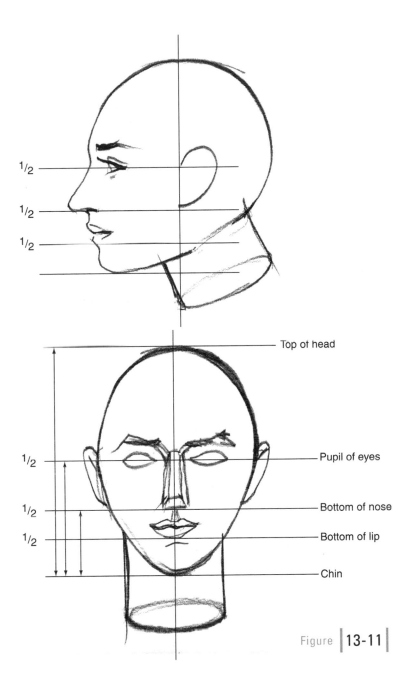

1/2

1/2

1/2

—— Top of head

1/2 —— Pupil of eyes

1/2 —— Bottom of nose

1/2 —— Bottom of lip

—— Chin

Figure | 13-11 |

cause the head is a rounded shape, what you're actually seeing are ellipses; remember that an ellipse from eye level appears as a straight line. If your eye level is below the head, the ellipses will curve downward; if your eye level is above the head they will curve upward, as shown in Figure 13-12. The more extreme the angle from which you view the head, the more rounded these ellipses will appear. If you draw what you think you know about the head, you'll probably draw it as if you were seeing it from eye level. Instead, make note of your eye level in relation to the head, and draw what you see using your understanding of elliptical perspective.

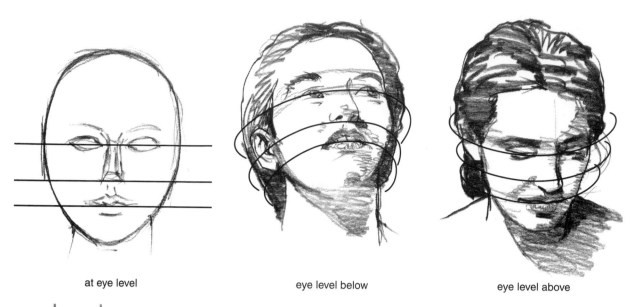

at eye level   eye level below   eye level above

Figure | 13-12 |

Linear perspective also affects your view of the head, depending on the angle from which you see it. If you're viewing the head in a three-quarters perspective, one eye will appear smaller than the other because it is farther away. Also, the other features will be affected, too. Always remember that things closest to you will be larger. It will also be a different shape from the nearer eye. Try to see the basic shapes in each feature, and then note how each shape changes depending on the angle from which you view it.

LANDSCAPE DRAWING

Many artists like to do landscape drawing because of the beauty of the subject matter and because it gets them outdoors especially when the weather is nice. At least outdoor views are more easily accessible to most people than are nude models! Even if you live in the heart of the city, you should be able to find a park or other green space nearby.

In your first attempts at landscape drawing, choose as your subject either a panoramic scene or a nearby vista that includes simple shapes with sharply defined edges such as rocks and trees. Something like a beautiful flower garden may draw your attention, but this would be difficult to draw in black and white. The local colors of the flowers are what give the garden its beauty. However, the values of those local colors are likely to be so close together that the garden loses its drama. It's not that such a drawing can't be done, but you'll be better starting off with an easier subject whose drama comes from clearly defined edges and textures rather than from color. It would be a shame to get so frustrated with your first few attempts at landscape drawing that you give it up altogether.

Framing the Picture

There's so much to see when you go outside that you may have trouble deciding how much of the great outdoors you want to draw. You have far fewer decisions to make when drawing a still life or a figure indoors; your subject is clearly delimited, and then you usually just draw what's directly behind it. Outdoors, even if you have chosen a specific subject matter, there's still a virtually unlimited amount of space all around that subject.

Figure | **13-13** |

That's why artists often use a framing device to help them compose their picture and block out the parts of the vista that they don't want to draw. Take a 6 × 9-inch piece of white cardboard and cut a rectangular hole in it, using the same proportions as your drawing pad. Holding the cardboard in your outstretched arm as in Figure 13-13, move it around until you like what you see in your frame. If you forget your cardboard frame, simply use your hands, as shown in Figure 13-14. Besides blocking out the part of the background you don't want to include in your drawing, you're also composing your picture as you move the cardboard or your hands around. You can't pick up the trees and bushes to move them where you want them, but you can remember the compositional principles of unity, focal point, and balance as you choose how to frame your picture. Later, as the drawing progresses to the stage where you create volume, you can use the white of the cardboard as a reference point in comparing values.

Seeing the Basic Shapes

The next step, after you've composed your picture, is to create an accurate line drawing

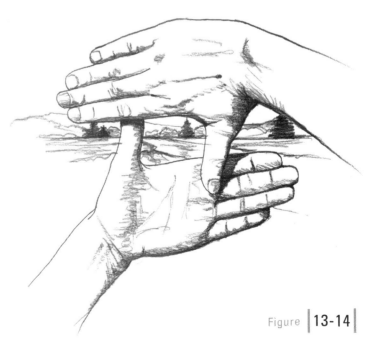

Figure | **13-14** |

Figure **13-15**

of what you see, just as in still-life drawing. As always, you start by visualizing your subject as a set of basic shapes. In nature, shapes and contours are irregular, and no two forms are identical. Nevertheless, you need to simplify each feature of the landscape into a set of basic shapes so you can draw it. There's no one basic shape that underlies every tree or every rock or every bush. In looking at a specific fallen tree, you may see a cone-shaped object while your friend may see a cylinder. After you each block in your basic shape, you'll each modify it in different ways to match what you're seeing. You may straighten the sides of your cone somewhat in this modification process, while your friend will be tapering the sides of his or her cylinder. Either way, you both started with a basic shape that helped you understand what you were seeing, and then modified it so that it more closely resembled the actual object.

A landscape like the one in Figure 13-15 looks intimidating at first. Looking from a rocky cliff, you see a panorama including mountains in the distance, foliage in the foreground, and flat rocks in the middle ground leading off into the mountains. Yet the very process of visualizing basic shapes and lightly sketching them on the paper, as in Figure 13-16, makes the subject much less intimidating. The rocks and mountains have distinct edges, which have been drawn

Figure **13-16**

as basic shapes in Figure 13-16 and then modified somewhat to match the actual landscape. Blocking in the shapes helps you see quickly how your drawing is going and allows you to adjust the shape, size, and position of each element; thus, it's a good idea to draw as lightly as possible when you start out.

After establishing a line drawing, you block in some tones as usual, as shown in Figure 13-17. Since foliage sometimes doesn't have distinct edges of light and dark, it can be hard to figure out how to block in the tones. Start with blocking in tone for the foreground, middle ground, and background. Then block in some tones indicating the foliage and any deep crevices in rocks. Don't worry about the texture of the leaves at this point, especially if they're small in relation to the rest of the drawing. Keep working over the whole drawing rather than trying to finish one area at a time. The sun is moving, so you have to work quickly. When you feel you have captured what-

Figure | **13-17** |

ever it was that made you want to draw this landscape, the drawing is complete. How much detail you want to include is up to you. Landscape drawing is about capturing a beautiful or dramatic outdoor setting on paper.

Creating the Illusion of Space

In landscape drawing, you have to create the illusion of space for distances that can be many miles, as opposed to the inches that separate objects in a typical still-life drawing. The principles of creating the illusion of space that you learned in Chapter 7 become more pronounced in landscape drawing. In the finished drawing in Figure 13-15, note how size, overlapping, placement, and the detail and value of objects have been used to create the illusion of great distance. The more extreme the use of these elements, the greater the distance that is created. The bushes in the foreground appear larger than the mountains in the background. The rocks in the middle ground overlap the mountains in the background. The mountains are placed higher in the picture plane than the features in the middle ground, which are in turn higher than the foreground objects. Finally, compare the level of value contrast and detail between the background, foreground, and middle ground. The mountains are virtually all the same value, and that value is close to that of the sky above them. There's greater value contrast in the cliff's edge in the middle ground, and even more in the bushes in the foreground. The bushes are rendered with such detail that you can see individual leaves, whereas the mountains show no detail at all.

Creating Volume

You create volume in landscapes, as in still lifes, by shading in light, shadow, and cast shadow areas. However, your task is complicated by the fact that your light source—the sun—is moving. You must work as quickly as possible to block in the tones; shadow patterns can change dramatically over the course of an hour or two, especially late and early in the day. Make note of the height and angle of the sun when you start the process of adding value to create the form. Then when the shadow patterns are slightly different a little later, you'll be able to use your understanding of the appearance of the form as it was when you started.

As usual, squint to see the shapes and values of the shadows, and move over your entire drawing filling in the basic values. Begin by seeing everything as simply light or dark without thinking of the exact value of gray. Keep the volume structures simple at first, particularly in any foliage. Remember the form of the underlying structure and, whatever you do, don't spend time trying to finish one object before moving to the next; you'll lose your light. You can fill in texture and details later. Do, however, pay attention to reflected light; in nature, there's light bouncing off every object in every direction. When you've taken a limited amount of time filling in the values, you'll have captured a sense of volume in your landscape.

Creating Texture

Everything in nature has its own texture, from the roughness of tree bark to the smoothness of the surface of a placid pond. Treat texture like a detail in your drawing, and begin to render the textures you see only after you have filled in the underlying volume structure of each object.

Drawing texture in an object gives it detail and therefore draws the eye toward it. The further away an object is, the less texture you can see. If you drew all the objects with equal texture, you would flatten out your picture plane. So don't get "texture happy"—draw in the texture near the end of your drawing, after you've established volume, and draw the texture in detail only for objects that are in the foreground.

When drawing leaves and blades of grass, for instance, you don't want to just keep making the same kind of leaves smaller and smaller as they move into the background. This would create a busy effect that would distract the viewer's eye. The appearance of the texture changes as it moves farther from your eye, as shown in Figure 13-18. By the time a bush reaches the middle ground, you can barely see individual leaves any more. Eventually, in the background, blended tones are enough to suggest the texture of the foliage. This simplification helps create the illusion of space in your drawing.

To render the texture of objects in the foreground, first closely observe the textures that you see. The texture of the tree illustrated in Figure 13-19, for instance, has a pronounced vertical pattern because of the roughness of the bark. Carefully observe the shape of the leaves, like those shown in Figure 13-20. Every tree and bush has a different kind of leaf, each of which gives a different texture; the maple leaves shown in Figure 13-20a have a very different texture from the pine needles in Figure 13-20b. Grass, on the other hand, grows

Figure | 13-18a

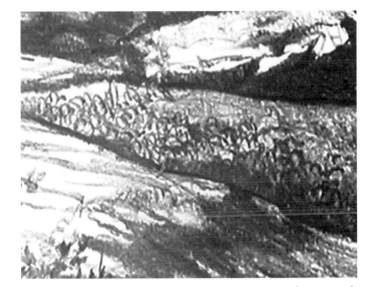

Figure | 13-18b

Figure | 13-18c

Figure | 13-19 |

Figure | 13-20a |

Figure | 13-20b |

up from the ground in an upright pattern, yet, when it gets long, the tops of the leaves can fall about in a haphazard texture, as shown in Figure 13-21. Rocks, too, like the ones shown in Figure 13-22, vary enormously in their textures; some are smooth, some are rough, and some have patterns cut into the surface.

Drawing Atmosphere

The weather affects the look of your drawing. On a sunny day, you can see for miles, and everything looks sharp and clear. A landscape drawing done on such a day (like the one you saw in Figure 13-15) has clean, distinct edges and a lot of contrast between light and dark ar-

Figure **13-21**

eas. Conversely, in humid or foggy weather, the water in the air creates a haze that acts like a filter, making everything look softer and less distinct. A drawing made on such a day, like the one in Figure 13-23, has soft edges in the background, with some areas being completely blended to show that they are obscured in mist. Notice how little detail you can see. Mist obscures and softens the details. On a cloudy day, the edges may be relatively sharp, but the contrast in values between light, shadow, and

Figure **13-22**

cast shadow areas will be less extreme than on a sunny day; the values stay closer to the middle of the gray scale. If you want to draw rain, just draw the landscape as you see it on a cloudy day and add the rain as a detail. Raindrops up close against a dark value can be drawn with the point of a kneaded eraser; remove the charcoal in vertical or diagonal dotted lines, depending on whether the wind is blowing the rain at an angle. If the raindrops are against a light value, draw light vertical or diagonal dotted lines with the charcoal or pencil. Be careful not to overdo the texture of the rain.

ARTISTIC SUCCESS

No matter what you draw, the key to artistic success is the same: simplify what you are seeing into basic shapes. Once you understand what you are seeing, you'll be able to draw it more easily. Your sighting and measuring techniques will help you to modify these basic shapes into ones more like the ones you are seeing. Then you add shading to give objects—still-life objects,

Figure **13-23**

the human figure, or features of landscape—their volume as the light reveals it. Finally, you add details to make your drawing come to life.

Anything worth doing takes practice. The more you draw, perhaps aided by additional instruction, the better an artist you will become as your skills increase. Be proud of your work, no matter where you are in your artistic learning curve. If you think a drawing you've made isn't particularly successful, take it as an opportunity to further hone your skills; we learn more from our mistakes than from our successes. At least you had the courage to "put pen to paper." Not everyone can say the same.

SUMMARY

With this brief introduction to figure and landscape drawing, your introductory drawing course is complete. Of course, if you want to master figures and landscapes, you'll want to take a more in-depth course specifically in those areas, devoting as much time to them as you did to still-life drawing in this book. Nevertheless, if you remember the basics—seeing the basic shapes and modifying them using sighting and measuring techniques, giving objects volume with gradations of tone—you can draw anything you see.

things to remember

- Figure and landscape drawing both use the same principles as still-life drawing.

- The best way to learn to draw the human figure is to draw nude models from life.

- Visualize the entire figure as a shape and place it on your page before you begin to draw.

- The human body is a collection of basic shapes consisting primarily of cylinders, modified spheres, and rectangles.

- Understanding the average or ideal human proportions will help you accurately draw the human form.

- Knowledge of anatomy is helpful in capturing the underlying structure of the human figure.

- The principle that distance and angle affects the appearance of the human figure is called *foreshortening.*

- Capturing the gesture is essential to giving life to a figure drawing.

- Drawing the hands, feet, and head requires additional practice on those areas, only because they are more complex than the body as a whole.

- Elliptical perspective affects the appearance of the head depending on your eye level.

- The best subjects for the beginning landscape artist are panoramic vistas or scenes including simple shapes with sharply defined edges.

- A cardboard frame, or one made with the hands, is useful in composing a landscape drawing.

- In landscape drawing, the use of size, overlapping, placement, detail, and value contrast to suggest the illusion of space must be more pronounced than in still-life drawing.

- When creating volume in a landscape drawing, first note the height and angle of the sun when you begin and then work as quickly as possible to block in basic tones before the sun moves too much.

- Natural objects have unique textures. Textures should be fully rendered only in objects that are in the foreground.

- The effect of the atmosphere on the view must be rendered in landscape drawing.

in review

1. Which of the four basic shapes predominates in the human figure?

2. How many heads high is the average or ideal human figure when standing?

3. What is the midpoint of the average standing human figure?

4. What are the two basic shapes found in the hands and feet?

5. What is foreshortening?

6. In addition to knowledge of the ideal proportions of the head, what techniques are used to capture an accurate likeness?

7. What tools can you use to frame your landscape picture in order to block out the areas you don't want to draw?

8. Why must you work quickly to block in shadow areas when working outdoors?

9. What is the effect of including richly detailed texture in an area of your drawing?

project

Take your charcoal and pad on the road! If possible, find a park or rural area that offers an interesting view of a variety of natural objects. If you're stuck indoors, look out your window; even a cityscape usually offers a few natural features such as trees and bushes. Frame your subject with a cardboard viewer as described in this chapter, and then draw, beginning by visualizing and sketching the basic shapes. Be sure to note the angle of the sun before you begin filling in the volume. Take two or three hours to complete a finished landscape.

homework

With your graphite pencils, practice your skills at drawing the human figure by copying the drawings of the "old masters." Go to the fine arts section of your local library to find books of works by Michelangelo, Da Vinci, Rubens, Ingres, Degas, or any great artist. Find four nude drawings and copy them exactly as you see them.

index